Celebrating an Authentic Passover Seder

A Haggadah for Home and Church

Joseph M. Stallings

Resource Publications, Inc.
San Jose, California

Editorial director: Kenneth Guentert
Managing editor: Elizabeth J. Asborno

Front cover photograph taken by Perry Chow.
Interior photographs taken by Perry Chow and Joseph M. Stallings.

Reprint Department
Resource Publications, Inc.
160 E. Virginia Street #290
San Jose, CA 95112-5876

Library of Congress Cataloging in Publication Data
Stallings, Joseph, 1928-
    Celebrating an authentic Passover seder : a Haggadah for home and church / Joseph M. Stallings.
        p.   cm.
    ISBN0-89390-275-6
    1. Passover—Christian observance.   I. Haggadah. English. 1994.   II. Title.
BV199.P25S73   1994
264′.9—dc20   93-41337

Printed in the United States of America

98 97 96 95 94 | 5 4 3 2 1

All biblical and Talmudic translations are the author's.

This book is lovingly dedicated
to Milton and Phyllis Shuch of Temple Emanu-El,
who guided my research, and
to Blessie and Ernie La Scola and Fran and Jim Bermudes of Holy Family,
who made the tradition of an annual community seder a reality.

Contents

III. *Haggadah Shel Pesach,* The Passover Seder

Diagrams

Introduction

This book contains an authentic Haggadah for use at Passover. It contains all fifteen divisions that make up the "order" of the seder. All of these sections are enclosed within distinct borders that separate them from the rest of the book. This was done out of great respect, reverence, and sincere love for the venerable tradition of the Haggadot because that tradition is very sacred to Jews. That sacred tradition must be sincerely honored and not thoughtlessly sullied. Unfortunately, many Jews find a Christian seder a blasphemy!

For Jews, Passover recalls century after century of ruthless persecutions. Because Passover usually occurs near or during Holy Week, it became a signal for Christians to attack Jews as "Christ killers"[1] and take malicious "revenge." Ignorant of the dietary law that prohibits the ingestion of any blood whatsoever, Christians wrongly accused and convicted Jews for murdering Christian children for their blood to be used in the making of Passover Matzah.

The Nazis were the inheritors of all those generations of Christians who blamed every serious malady on the Jews, and they knew that most Europeans would not interfere with their "Final Solution"—"Ha-Shoah," the Holocaust—because they were simply and efficiently carrying out a sacrosanct tradition. When Jewish fami-

lies bravely opened their doors to welcome the prophet
Elijah to their seder, they were too often met by religious
fanatics who burst in to loot the house and seriously
brutalize the whole family, if not murder them all. There
are many alive today who escaped the death camps only
to live out the memory of that horror, to carry the guilt
of having survived when six million perished, and to
remain branded for life with the tattooed numbers on
their arms.

In families where all these memories remain, the happy
greeting of the prophet Elijah is followed by serious
maledictions against a Christendom that permitted if
not perpetrated all these atrocities.

> Pour out your wrath upon the nations who have not
>   known You
>   and upon the kingdoms who have not called upon
>   Your Name.
> Because they have devoured Jacob
>   and laid waste to his dwelling place (Ps 79:6,7).
>
> Pour out your wrath upon them
>   and let the anger of Your Face seize them.
> Let their home be made desolate
>   and let no one dwell in their tents (Ps 69:25,26).

However, the persecution of the Jews originally began
after the early Christians abandoned their annual observance of Passover in the fourth century and severed the
observance of Easter from the Jewish calendar.

By restoring the celebration of Passover to the Christian
community and by joining together in the Exodus from
Egypt, Jews and Christians can stop the writing of those
awful pages of history and instead prepare the whole
world for the coming kingdom and age of the Messiah.

The Passover Sacrifice

The Passover sacrifice was unique. Instead of the Levites in the Inner Court, laymen sacrificed the paschal
lambs in the Outer Courts of the Temple. Josephus

records that 256,500 lambs were sacrificed on one Passover (Josephus, *Wars of the Jews*, VI, 9, 3 [424]) and the Mishnah states that the paschal offering was made in three divisions, called "Assembly," "Congregation," and "Israel" ("Pesachim," 64b). It took three men to sacrifice each lamb. One man acted as the ritual slaughterer, called the "Shochet," who severed the animal's throat while the other two men held it suspended from a rod placed across their shoulders so that all of the blood could be drained from it. A priest caught the blood in a large basin made of silver or gold. When full, the basin containing the paschal lamb's blood was passed up a long line of priests until it reached the priests stationed in the Inner Court of the Holy Temple. These priests took the basins and flung the blood against the sides of the great altar of sacrifice. At the same time, the ritual slaughterer skinned the animal, opened its belly and removed the animal's kidneys, which he gave to the priest for a burnt offering that was conducted after the Passover sacrifice (Babylonian Talmud, "Pesachim," Mishnah 64a,b).

With the sacrificed lamb hung across the shoulders of one of them, the three men returned from the Temple to the place where the lamb would be eaten. The animal was then washed thoroughly with water and completely salted to draw off the remaining blood. Then the men thrust a spit of pomegranate wood into the animal's mouth, through the carcass, and out the buttocks. The hind legs were stretched and tied to the spit. A shorter wooden spit was placed across the lamb's shoulders and the forelegs were stretched out to the sides and attached to it. The lamb's internal organs were washed, salted, and attached to the spits. Then the whole was placed over a bed of hot coals and roasted until the flesh was done and easy to remove (Babylonian Talmud, "Pesachim," Mishnah 74a).

The women were responsible for preparing the other two sacrificial elements, the unleavened bread and the bitter herbs. The Matzot had to be made and baked as quickly as possible, each batch taking less than a half-hour. Among the other foods for the supper, they prepared a popular puree of fruit and wine called "Charoset," which means "clay." Although traditional, some did not consider Charoset an obligation, while others did.

The Mishnah records that although some considered the Charoset as not compulsory, Rabbi Eleazar, son of Rabbi Zadok, said that it was compulsory, and in Temple times they used to place the roasted flesh of the Passover Lamb before him (Babylonian Talmud, "Pesachim," Mishnah 114a).

A Christian Seder

This is a Haggadah for use by Christians at home and at church. It will aid in the restoration of the equally devout observation of Passover that we Christians inherited from the time of the Apostles until we were forbidden to do so in the fourth century by the Roman emperor, Constantine. All of the Christian additions and addendum appear on separate pages or in footnotes, to clearly differentiate them from the traditional text.

Christians should become familiar with the seder because it authentically defines so much of what we do at Eucharist and Holy Communion. Christians should be especially informed about the observance of Passover at the time of the Temple because the Last Supper defines who we really are.[2] Without such an understanding, we have only a faint idea of what is meant by John's "Behold the Lamb of God!" (Jn 1:29,36) and Paul's "Christ was sacrificed for us as our Passover" (1 Cor 5:7).

זִכָּרוֹן/
ANAMNHΣIΣ

Zikaron-Anamnesis

Primarily, we all must become reacquainted with the Jewish concept of the "Zikaron." The seder is a Zikaron today, and the Passover supper at the time of Temple was a Zikaron. The Septuagint and New Testament use two Greek words to translate "Zikaron" ("mnemosunon" in Ex 12:14 and "anamnesis" in 1 Cor 11:24,25);

neither of these adequately conveys the real meaning of the unique concept of "Zikaron" because the Greeks relived mythological legends while the Jews relived historical events. At an authentic Passover service, you are not "remembering" the events of an ancient past; all of those events are brought into the present by the ritual of the Zikaron so that you actually participate in them.

Looking closely at the verse in Exodus 13:8, "And *you shall relate*[3] to your child on that day, saying, This is because of what the LORD (YHWH) did to *me* when *I came out from Egypt*." It was determined that since "You shall relate" is a commandment of Torah, it follows that each person must recognize that he or she personally came out from Egypt. No matter how many generations or millennia removed all of us may be from the events of the Exodus, *at the Passover supper, the LORD (YHWH) brings each one of us out from Egypt together with Moses and the children of Israel!* (Babylonian Talmud, "Pesachim" Mishnah, 116a). This is the accurate definition of "Zikaron."

Jesus twice reaffirmed this Jewish concept at the Last Supper. At the "Ha-Motzi"—the Breaking of Bread— and after the Supper, he said over the bread and the wine, "Do this as my Zikaron ("Poíeite eis ten emen *anamnesin*"; 1 Cor 11:24,25). In spite of the Scripture scholars' failure to translate Christ's words accurately, no matter how many generations or millennia separate us from that great event, we are not "remembering" what Jesus did at the Last Supper; *we have been gathered by the Lord to share that same supper with him and the first disciples within that upper room in Jerusalem!* That is in fact what "Do this as my Anamnesis" means.

A Kingdom of Priests and a Holy Nation

A Kingly Priesthood, A Holy Nation

מַמְלֶכֶת כֹּהֲנִים וְגוֹי קָדוֹשׁ

ΒΑΣΙΛΕΟΝ ΙΕΠΤΕΥΜΑ ΕΘΟΣ ΑΓΙΟΝ

Echoing God's proclamation to the children of Israel in Exodus 19:6, St. Peter calls Christians "A kingly priest-hood, a holy nation" (1 Pt 2:9). What image did St. Peter have in mind? He had the vivid memory of the Passover sacrifice and supper at the time of the Holy Temple imbedded in his writing. According to eyewitnesses such as the philosopher Philo and the chroniclers of the Mishnah, laymen did the actual sacrifice of the paschal lambs in the outer courts of the Temple. Since they were elevated to the dignity of the priesthood, the men had to first immerse themselves in the ritual bath, called a "Mikveh"[4], and put on the white linen robes and hats of the priests before entering the Temple with their lambs. Since three men were required to sacrifice each lamb and there were over 200,000 paschal lambs offered each Passover, over 600,000 men entered the Temple on the 14th of Nisan as priests (Josephus, *Antiquities* XVII.9.3[213]). The church historian Eusebius records that the Apostle John continued to wear the priest's hat as he conducted the Passover supper on the 14th/15th of Nisan until his death. Moreover, John's image of "washed in the Blood of the Lamb" in Revelation was invoked by the impressive sight of the men returning from the Temple with their white robes soaked with the blood of their paschal lamb. Christians continued to wear the white linen robes of the priests as they were immersed in the Mikveh at baptism[5] because they were a "kingly priesthood and a holy nation."

However, it was not only the men who entered the Holy Temple to sacrifice the paschal lambs who bathed in the Mikveh and wore the robes of the priests; all of those men, women, and children who ate the Passover supper also had to bathe in the ritual bath and put on white linen robes. They were elevated to the priesthood as well so that they could eat the Passover supper.

Passover was also unique because at all other commu-nion sacrifices, the priests kept part of the animal offered in the Temple for their own suppers (Lv 7:33; 10:14) while the laity ate the remaining portions at home. At Passover, however, everyone was a priest and therefore were privileged to eat the entire animal, which was comprised of the roasted head, body and legs at the supper and the roasted inner organs at the hors d'oeuvres of the meal (Ex 12:9).

There was more to it than simply eating the entire roasted lamb at Passover. By all sharing in the consumption of the roasted flesh[6] of the Passover sacrifice at the sacrificial supper, *each man, woman and child directly participated in that Passover sacrifice.* What does that mean today to us, the kingly priesthood of all believers? It means that *at Holy Communion every man, woman and child shares directly in the one perfect Passover sacrifice of our Lord, Jesus Christ, on Calvary* (1 Cor 10:16-18).

Christ Was Also Sacrificed for Us As Our Passover

ΚΑΙ ΓΑΡ ΤΟ ΠΑΣΧΑ ΗΜΩΝ ΥΠΕΡ ΗΜΩΝ ΕΤΥΘΗ ΧΡΙΣΤΟΣ

Saint Paul on Proper Passover Observance:

Do you not know that a little leaven will leaven the whole lump of dough? Therefore, purge out the old leaven that you may be a new lump as you are unleavened bread! *Christ was sacrificed for us as our Passover* so that we should celebrate the Feast not with the old leaven, the leaven of malice and wickedness but with the Unleavened Bread of sincerity and truth (1 Cor 5:6-8).

St. Paul's words echo the ancient Jewish tradition of searching the house for the last bits of leaven and burning it. Leaven, "Chametz" in Hebrew, was regarded by the rabbis as a symbol of our "evil inclinations" or "Yetzer Hara." Such old and spoiled leaven could corrupt the whole dough of life. St. Paul calls that old Chametz the leaven of malice and wickedness. Out of this belief came the ritual of cleaning the house thoroughly before Passover. At the conclusion of the venerable tradition of spring cleaning on the day before

Passover, Mother would leave some bread crumbs in little piles in each room. Then, on the night before Passover, Father, assisted by the eldest son, searched each room by lamplight or candlelight, first reciting:

Blessed are You, O LORD our God,
    the king of the universe.
You have sanctified us through the observance of
    Your commandments
and commanded us concerning the removal of
    Chametz.

Then, by the light of the son's lamp or candle (a flashlight today), Father brushes the offending crumbs he finds in each room onto a wooden (or paper) plate, using a large feather. When all of the rooms have been searched, Father carefully wraps the plate, feather, and collected bread crumbs in a cloth so that nothing can fall out. Then Father and son recite the following:

All the leaven and leavened items in my possession
    that I have not seen nor have I removed
Be considered as not to exist
    and regarded as simply the dust of the earth!

Father and son carefully set the wrapped cloth aside overnight; after breakfast the next morning Father takes the cloth containing the collected Chametz outside the house, where the son has prepared a fire. Placing the package upon the fire so that it completely burns up, Father recites:

All of the leaven and leavened items in my possession
    Whether I have seen them or not
    Whether I have removed them or not
Are to be considered as not to exist
    and regarded as simply the dust of the earth!

Passover, therefore, is not just another holy day. It is always a new beginning and a conscious reactualization (Zikaron-Anamnesis) of who we really are.

Because this introduction and Haggadah cannot explain in detail all of the significance of the modern seder, and it can only introduce the subject of the Passover sacrifice at the time of the Holy Temple, I sincerely recommend that you read my book on just these subjects, *Rediscovering Passover* (Resource Publications, Inc., 1988).

Notes

1. The Romans killed Jesus. By accepting the people's welcome of him as "King of Israel" (Jn 12:13), Christ broke the Roman law of *lex julia majestatis,* which made it a capital crime against the authority of the emperor for anyone to be declared a king without imperial sanction. The Romans posted the reason for Jesus' crucifixion on a sign at the top of his cross: "Jesus of Nazareth, King of the Jews."

2. Many scholars do not believe that the Last Supper was Passover. They base their erroneous belief on their misreading of John 18:24 and 19:14. John 18:24 refers only to the chief priests and elders of the Sanhedrin, who had an additional seven days of Passover suppers beginning on the 15th/16th of Nisan (Josephus, *Antiquities* III.12.5[249]). "Preparation day" meant Friday in the first century and was never used in reference to the 14th of Nisan, which was always called "The Feast of Passover." Josephus also uses "preparation day" to signify the day before the Sabbath (*Antiquities* XVI.6.2[163]), but he never uses "preparation day" in his numerous references to the 14th of Nisan. John 19:14 should be translated, "Friday of Passover Week."

3. The Hebrew verb for "you shall relate" is "Haggidta," and it is from this verb in the verse of Exodus 13:8 that the name "Haggadah" is derived. The Haggadah is the manual for use at the seder.

4. Archaeologists have uncovered around the Temple area some forty "Mikva'ot" that were used by those entering the sacred precincts. Many more have been uncovered in private homes of the period.

5. Such a Mikveh was discovered in a second-century church in Duros Europa.

6. The separate English and Greek words for "body," "flesh" and "meat" are all the same word in Hebrew. That one Hebrew word is "BaSaR" (בָּשָׂר) and the same word in Aramaic "Bisra" (בִּשְׂרָא).

Part I

HOW TO PREPARE AND PRESENT AN AUTHENTIC PASSOVER SEDER

At Home

Choosing the Date

We have learned over the years that the best time to begin planning for Passover is at the beginning of Lent. That observation has remained true whether we were planning a seder at home or for 150 people in the community center at church. Thus, your first decision when planning your seder is the date. Ideally, a Christian observance of Passover should be held on Holy Thursday, as this is the commemoration of the Last Supper. For us, however, that has too often proved to be impossible; there is so much going on at church that it simply leaves no time for the addition of a seder. The Monday and Tuesday of Holy Week were much better choices for a community seder, and Palm Sunday has turned out to be the best day for our home celebration.

Since it is the Jewish tradition to observe two nights of Passover, you may wish to plan one seder at home early in Holy Week for your "first night," and then attend the public seder at your church or at a local temple for the "second night." Keep in mind, though, that reservations at your church or at temple are required; additionally, at temple the strict kosher dietary rules are observed, such as no mixing of meat and dairy products at the same meal and no using leavening agents in food preparation.

Making the Guest List

Although you may want to invite as many guests as possible to observe Passover at your home, you cannot cram so many around your table that there is no elbow room. Besides eating the ritual foods and the dinner you have prepared, everyone needs space to hold and turn the pages of their Haggadah or Passover manual during the ritual. Each person must have a Haggadah to read from.

Planning the Meal

Once your guest list is complete, carefully plan the meal. The ritual foods are easy, as they are traditional and the amount is determined by the number of family members and guests. It is best to prepare them the day before in order to give you plenty of time to set the table, prepare the meal, and visit before you seat everyone. Remember, it may take from one hour to one-and-a-half hours, sometimes longer, from the time you begin the seder to when you actually serve the dinner. Therefore, all of the cold food will have to stay in the refrigerator and all of the hot food in the oven, on hotplates, or in crockpots until served! Casseroles are best, especially if guests are bringing some of the dishes.

Recipes for the ritual foods begin on page 22; recipes for the Passover dinner begin on page 27.

Preparing the Seder Table

Passover is the preeminent feast of the Bible, and you will want to set your family table with your best. It is the Holy Day of all Holy Days. In addition to the beautiful tablecloth, dishes, glasses, and silverware, you will also need the following:

☐ At least two candles and candle sticks

☐ A seder plate or a very large platter

☐ A plate and a Matzah cover or three napkins

☐ An extra plate to serve the Matzah

☐ A white napkin for the Afikoman

☐ A large bowl, pitcher of water, and two guest towels

☐ A large goblet for the Elijah Cup

☐ A Kiddush Cup for Father

☐ Small 3-ounce glasses for everyone

☐ Small bowls of salt water for dipping

☐ A Haggadah for each person

☐ Some cushions placed on Father's chair

Candles

At the time of Christ, brass and clay lamps filled with olive oil were used to light the room for Sabbath meals and holy day suppers. Candles came into use many centuries later. Although we use candles on our seder table now, the traditional blessing says, "...and commands us to light the Holy Day lights," to remind us that lamps were used to light the Passover suppers in the holy city of Jerusalem while the holy temple was still in existence.

It has always been the tradition for mothers and wives to light the lamps and candles before the Sabbath and holy day meals. The bible says, "These women also followed him when he was in Galilee and ministered to him. And there were many other women who had come up with him to Jerusalem" (Mk 15:41) to celebrate Passover. Jesus' mother, Mary, was among these women (Jn 19:25-27) and custom would demand that she would lead the others in the blessing of the holy day lights.

Seder Plate

I consider the seder plate an important relic from our past. Large brass and stone platters were used at the Last Supper to serve the whole roasted paschal lambs to the diners (Mk 14:12-16). Families purchased those platters for use on their Passover tables in the holy city and then took them with them when they returned home. The large platters were used by the family every year, whether they made the pilgrimage to Jerusalem or observed the alternate form of the Passover ritual at home where they were unable to eat the roasted flesh of the sacrificed lamb. These religious objects remained in their family for years. Moreover, families did not discard the platters after the holy temple was destroyed and the Passover sacrifice abolished; rather, they continued to place the platters on their seder tables and

Seder Plate

arrange upon them mementoes of the pilgrimage to Jerusalem and the paschal suppers they ate there.

We do the same thing today. We remember the Passover sacrifice at the time of Christ by placing the "Z'roa," a roasted lamb bone, in the center of our seder plate. Above and to the left of the Z'roa, we place the "Baytzah," or roasted egg, as a symbol of our mourning the loss of the holy temple and its Passover sacrifices. Of course, a dish of the important "Maror" must also be placed upon the seder plate, above and to the right of the Z'roa. The dish can contain either sliced or pureed horseradish, a very bitter herb indeed. Concerning the Passover sacrifice, the bible commands, "And on this night they shall eat its flesh roasted by fire, and they shall eat it with unleavened bread and bitter herbs" (Ex 12:8). We place "Chazeret," Romaine lettuce, and "Karpas," a small bunch of parsley, on the plate as a memorial of the first course of the Last Supper. The hors d'oeuvres of that meal consisted of the roasted giblets of the paschal lambs. The giblets were served on beds of Romaine lettuce and assorted springtime vegetables such as scallions and celery. The giblets and vegetables were wrapped in the Romaine lettuce leaves and dipped into bowls of salt water and herb-flavored vinegar. A small bowl of "Charoseth" is also placed upon the seder plate. This puree of fruit, raisins, nuts, honey and wine was very popular at the time of Christ. Jesus identified his betrayer as "that one is he to whom I give the morsel that I have dipped" (Jn 13:26). The bowl into which Jesus dipped that bit of food to give to Judas is believed to have contained the popular Charoseth.

Matzah Cover and Extra Plate

During the ritual, it is traditional to place three "Matzoth" in the three pockets in this cover. Matzah covers are very large, much larger than the store-bought Matzah we place into them today. Whether they are square or round, these large covers recall the large sheets of unleavened bread that were used during the ritual at the time of Christ.

We continue to place three Matzoth in them for two reasons. Passover is the first and foremost feast of the bible, "This month shall be for you the first of your months; it shall be for you the beginning month of the year" (Ex 12:2).

> "Today you are going out [from Egypt], in this month of Abib (Spring). And when the LORD brings you into the land of the Canaanites, the Hittites, the Amorites, the Hivites, and the Jebusites, which He swore to your Fathers He would give to you, a land flowing with milk and honey, you shall observe this rite [of Passover] in this month (Ex 13:4,5).

Therefore, Passover must be honored by the serving of three loaves of bread for the meal, just as the Sabbath is honored by serving two loaves in remembrance of the extra "Manna" that was gathered on Friday by the children of Israel in the wilderness for eating on the Sabbath: "And it was on the sixth day that they gathered double the bread, two omers for each one" (Ex 16:22,23).

The three loaves of unleavened bread also represent the three classes of Jews at the time of Christ. One loaf represents the hereditary class of priests. It is called "Kohen," which is the Hebrew word for "priest." The second is called "Levy" and is named after the Levites, who served the priests in the Temple. The Levites were the original "Teachers of the Law" to the Jewish people. But after the conquests of Alexander the Great, the Levites became influenced by Greek culture and mixed Judaism with Greek philosophy and Greek customs. The majority of the Jews turned against them as adulterers of the true faith and a group of laymen called scribes resisted the Greek influence and replaced the Levites as teachers of the Law. By separating themselves from the authority of the priests and Levites, who were Sadducees, these scribes and their followers became known as the Pharisees or "Separatists." The third loaf is called "Yisrael" and represents the people, the Israelites.

White Napkin   Since the time of Christ, that last thing to be eaten at the Passover supper is the "Afikoman. While the Temple existed, this Afikoman was a small sandwich made with a piece of the Passover lamb, "the size of an olive," and some horseradish placed between two pieces of unleavened bread. This sandwich was consumed at the conclusion of the supper and then an acclamation was recited that all of the laws, traditions, and customs of the Passover had been met (Ex 12:8-10). For the very poor, this morsel of roasted meat may have been the only flesh of the sacrificed Passover lamb they could afford. They would have had to substitute other roast meat, called "Chaggigah" or "Festival Offering," which was usually donated by organizations set up to guarantee that the poor had wine and food for their celebrations. Nowadays, only Matzah is eaten as the Afikoman.

The custom of wrapping the Matzah set aside for the Afikoman is ancient. It was inspired by the passage, "And the people took up their dough before it was leavened, and bound their kneading troughs in their clothes and placed them upon their shoulders" (Ex 12:34). The cloth wrapped around the Matzah represents that clothing wrapped around the kneading bowls of the Israelites, which they carried on their shoulders during their hurried flight out of Egypt.

For Christians there is an even more poignant significance to this ceremony. It is the second of the three Matzot that is "broken for us." That phrase would be suggestive of the Second Person of the Trinity. The cloth wrapped around it, then, would intimate the burial shroud of Jesus. The returning of the Afikoman to the Matzah cover, or to a hiding place, could imply the entombment of Christ. Its return to the table for the conclusion of the supper would then symbolize the resurrection. I am convinced that this ritual was practiced by Christians at their seders in the first centuries. They observed Passover on the 14th of the Jewish month, Nisan, as the feast of the resurrection until persecutions by the Romans forced them to a Sunday observance. The original name for Easter was "Pascha," which in fact means "Passover."

Bowls of Water and Towels

Unique to the Passover supper is the requirement to wash our hands twice. It recalls that the Last Supper was served in two courses. Everyone had to wash their hands before eating the hors d'oeuvres and then they had to wash again before the breaking of bread, which was the blessing and sharing of the Matzah at the "Motzi-Matzah," which began the formal meal.

Bowls of Water for Washing

Moreover, "Look at Israel according to the flesh; are not those who eat the sacrifices a fellowship of partakers in the altar?" (1 Cor 10:18). Ordinary people could share in all of the other communion sacrifices by setting aside prescribed portions of their offerings, which were given to the priests (Lv 7:33,34). But in order to be eligible to eat the entire paschal lamb (Ex 12:9), including the priestly portions, everyone had to be elevated to the dignity of the priesthood. An obligatory rite of purification, then, was the reason for everyone immersing their whole bodies in the "Mikveh," or "ritual bath" (Jn 13:10).

Elijah Cup

Four cups of wine are required at the Passover supper, based upon the four promises:

> Therefore, say to the Children of Israel, I Am the LORD! [1.] I will bring you out from under the burdens of Egypt, [2.] I will deliver you from their slavery, [3.] I will redeem you with an arm outstretched and with great judgments, [4.] I will take you as a people for Myself and I will be your God (Ex 6:6,7).

But there was a problem. Were their only four promises, or did "I will be your God" constitute a fifth? If so, a fifth cup would be necessary. The sages of Israel could never decide. So they decreed that a fifth cup be poured during the supper, but no one should drink from it. They hoped that the prophet Elijah would solve the problem for them when he came during Passover to announce the arrival of the Messiah. This persistent hope gave this fifth cup its name, the Elijah Cup.

Kiddush Cup

In Jewish homes, it is customary to supply Father with a special glass or small ornate chalice. He pronounces the "Kiddush" or "Blessing of the Fruit of the Vine" over this special cup at every Sabbath and holy day supper. He will then bless the Sabbath or the feast day. The Kiddush may be sung or recited, and it is customary to do so in Hebrew.

The Kiddish for Passover was already well established by the time of Christ. The first two blessings, over the wine and over the feast, are mentioned in the "Mishnah." These blessings in Hebrew were certainly recited or sung by Jesus at the Last Supper. Among the furnishings the disciples found in the upper room (Mk 14:15) was a large metal or ceramic container of water set over a brazier of burning coals placed in the middle of the room. It was there to supply the hot water that must be mixed with the four cups to make the wine kosher and palatable. Jesus followed the religious requirement of mixing water with the wine in a large urn for each of the four cups. The disciples then took this urn from table to table and ladled some of this wine Jesus had blessed into each person's goblet or cup. When everyone's cup was filled, they all repeated the blessing and drank their wine.

Small Wine Glasses

Since four cups of wine must be drunk at Passover, and yet sobriety must be maintained throughout the service, it is customary to supply each person with a small glass. That allows them to finish each of the required glasses without any feelings of giddiness. The host should also advise everyone at the beginning of the service that the four cups must be emptied, and therefore, judgment should be used in the amount of wine they put into their glasses.

Cushions for Father's Chair

Everyone reclined on couches at the Last Supper (Jn 13:12). In spite of the fact of the Roman's cruel occupation of their nation, Passover remained the feast of freedom. It was the reliving of Exodus, that great liberation from slavery in Egypt. As a symbol of that redemption, the ritual required that they all recline on couches as a sign that they were actually free men and women. It was not an empty gesture, however, because they believed that the Lord would liberate them again, especially when the Messiah came to set them free.

People no longer recline on couches when they dine. But the cushions on Father's chair remind us that those who ate the Passover supper in the holy city of Jerusalem while the Temple existed were required to do so.

Setting the Seder Table

Set your table for the holy day that Passover is. Place the candles upon their candlesticks in the center of your table. Put a beautiful arrangement of flowers between them. Place the seder plate, or large platter, between this centerpiece and the head of the table. Starting at the top, in relation to where Father sits, place the following items upon the seder plate:

- ☐ a roasted lamb shank or bone in the center

- ☐ the top of a horseradish root or small bowl of ground horseradish to the upper right

- ☐ a bowl of Charoset below the horseradish

- ☐ a small container of salt at the bottom

- ☐ a bunch of parsley (and/or lettuce, celery, scallions) to the left of the salt

- ☐ a roasted egg on the upper left

Place the large empty goblet for the Elijah cup near the seder plate. To Father's left, put the plate covered by the Matzah cover. Put a single Matzah in each pocket of the Matzah cover, or stack three Matzot upon the plate and place a napkin on top of each one. The rest of the Matzot may be put on one or two plates, set aside for later, and brought to the table with dinner. It is the only bread permitted at Passover (Ex 12:15).

To Father's right, place another white napkin to wrap the Afikoman and an extra plate to be used to serve the Matzah. Put a small wine glass at each person's place setting, and if he has one, a Kiddish Cup at Father's place. (There is also a custom of placing another Kiddish Cup at the eldest son's place and one at Mother's place.) It is also the custom to place all of the glasses at

Father's setting in the beginning so that he can pour the first glass for everyone.

Matches, and possibly a taper, are placed at Mother's setting for the candle-lighting ceremony. The bowl, pitcher, and towels may be placed at Mother's setting— if there is room—or on a side table. Everyone has a small salad plate placed upon their dinner plate as an individual seder plate. A small piece of roast lamb is placed in the center and surrounded by a generous tablespoon of Charoset, a small teaspoon of horseradish, a single sprig of parsley, a roasted egg and a small teaspoon of salt (kosher salt if possible). Place the small bowls of salt water around the table so that they are within easy reach of everyone. Bottles or carafes of wine, kosher for Passover, and/or carafes of grape juice, are placed conveniently on the table to fill all of the glasses for the first two of the four cups of the "Fruit of the Vine." The remaining two glasses of the four cups will be served after dinner.

Recipes for the Ritual Foods

The following foods are to be eaten as part of the seder ritual (as opposed to your seder dinner). Plan your purchasing well ahead because lamb, kosher wine, and Matzah become scarce as Passover and Easter approach. For my family, I go ahead of time to a butcher and order a whole leg of lamb with the shank attached, which will be placed upon our seder plate. When I pick up the lamb, I also purchase three or four lamb chops; at least one box of Matzot; two bunches of parsley; enough eggs so that there is one for each person's seder plate and one for the large seder plate; kosher salt; apples; almonds; walnuts; raisins; honey and cinnamon for the Charoset; one horseradish root and some fresh beets for the Maror (or several bottles of kosher horseradish, red in color, prepared for Passover); and five or six bottles of kosher wine and grape juice for the ritual and two bottles of a dinner wine for our meal.

Basic Charoset or "Clay"

2 apples, peeled and cut into quarters (put in
water to keep from coloring)

½ cup almonds

½ cup walnuts

1 cup raisins

½ lemon with rind

¼ cup sweet red wine

2 Tablespoons honey

1 teaspoon cinnamon

Put the almonds, walnuts, raisins, lemon with rind, sweet wine, honey and cinnamon in a food processor. Chop together until they becomes a smooth puree. Add the apples one quarter at a time, just coarse chopping them. You want the apples to remain in small pieces. Place the Charoset in a bowl, cover it tightly and refrigerate overnight.

The Stallings Family's Favorite Charoset

4 apples, pared and quartered (placed in
water until used)

1 cup pitted dates

1 cup raisins

½ cup almonds

½ cup walnuts

½ lemon with peel

1 Tablespoon fresh ginger slices

1 Tablespoon ground cinnamon

3 whole cloves, crushed

½ to 1 cup sweet red wine

¼ cup honey

Put dates, half of the raisins, almonds, walnuts, lemon with peel, fresh ginger, cinnamon, clove nails, half the wine, and the honey in food processor and blend thoroughly into a puree. Add the remaining half-cup wine and blend. Add the apples one quarter at a time and the raisins and coarsely chop. It should have the consistency of mud, as it represents the clay out of which the Israelites made bricks in Egypt. Put the Charoset in a tightly covered bowl and refrigerate overnight.

A tablespoon of Charoset will be placed on each person's individual seder plate, and a small bowl of it on the main seder plate.

At our house, the leftover Charoset is used to make our Easter baklava. The baklava is made the usual way with layers of filo dough, but the leftover Charoset is spread over the center sheet, then the remaining layers of filo dough are stacked on top.

Maror or "Passover Horseradish"

1 fresh horseradish root, about 2 cups

2 whole, cooked beets, peeled

1 teaspoon salt

2 Tablespoon sugar

½ to ¾ cup white wine vinegar

Wash the horseradish root thoroughly by scrubbing with a vegetable brush. Cut off the top and set aside for placing upon the seder plate. Carefully peel the rest of the root, cut into 1" ovals, then cut these in half. Put one third of this into the food processor with the peeled beets, salt, sugar, and white wine vinegar. Run processor until the root is chopped up. Add more root and chop again. Add the rest of the root and more white vinegar if necessary. Run the processor until it all becomes a paste. Remove the lid very carefully—it can take your breath away! Place the horseradish in a very tightly covered bowl and refrigerate overnight. Be careful when you remove the lid the next day; if you get it too close to your face, your eyes will water and you will choke up and gasp for air.

If this preparation is too much of a hazard to your health, and you can't use that much anyway, you can purchase the horseradish, kosher for Passover, in small jars at the supermarket.

One half to 1 teaspoon of horseradish is placed upon each person's individual seder plate. The top of the horseradish root is placed upon the main seder plate.

The leftover horseradish keeps very well in small jars in the refrigerator. We often find ourselves with a year supply.

Roast Eggs

If there are 12 people at your seder, you will roast 13 eggs—one for each person and one for your seder plate. Carefully place all of the eggs in a pan or casserole dish so they do not crack. Place the eggs in a cold oven and set at 200°. Roast them for 1½ hours. Then raise the temperature to 300° and continue roasting for 30 minutes more (do not start them at 300° or the some of the eggs might explode). The eggs are done when little brown spots appear on the shells. If the majority of the eggs do not have these spots, continue cooking until they do appear on most of the eggs. Remove them from the oven and cool, then refrigerate overnight.

One roasted egg will be placed upon each person's individual seder plate and a single egg on the main seder plate.

If your family and guests do not eat all of their eggs, they can be refrigerated and used in any egg dish. The one left on the seder plate can have its spots scrubbed off with water and a stiff brush, then colored for Easter.

Lamb Morsels

Besides the leg of lamb and its shank, 3 or 4 lean lamb chops may be purchased as well. Season them with salt and roast or broil until done. Cool completely. Then cut them into bite-size pieces, "the size of an olive."

One piece will be placed on each person's seder plate.

The custom in our family and at our church is to put toothpicks into these pieces to form a cross. The obvious reference is to the Lamb of God. But the Passover lambs were actually roasted on two spits of pomegranate wood that did form a cross. The longer piece went through the body and the hind legs were attached to it, while the smaller piece was placed across the shoulders and the two forelegs were stretched out and attached to it. Then the whole thing was placed over a bed of hot coals and roasted.

Parsley, Lettuce, Celery or Scallions

Whatever you use for the Karpas (parsley is preferred) must be thoroughly washed. The best way is to fill a sink with cold water and to plunge the bunches of parsley into the water several times until all the dirt and sand are flushed out. Set the bunch or bunches aside to drain, and then place in a plastic bag and refrigerate overnight.

A single sprig of parsley will be placed upon each person's seder plate and a small bunch upon the main seder plate.

Matzah

If you want to try your hand at making Matzah, the following recipe will help. In Hebrew school, teachers and students try to outrace each other in Matzah production. 28 minutes is considered a winning time.

> 2 pounds unbleached all-purpose flour
>
> 1½ cups water

Preheat oven to 500°.

Mix and knead the flour and water together until a firm dough is formed. Divide the dough into 8 pieces and roll out each piece into a circle about 8" around. Puncture the round with a fork, in a traditional design if you wish. Place the rounds on cookie sheets and bake 10 to 15 minutes in the hot oven until lightly brown. Archaeologists have discovered metal pans for baking Passover Matzah that have many holes cut into them for quick crusting, much like some pizza pans sold today.

Mozel Tov. Good Luck.

Recipes for Passover Dinner

For your Passover dinner, you may use the following recipes, which represent a typical Passover dinner at the Stallings' home.

- -

Passover Roast Lamb, Our Chaggigah

1 whole leg of lamb with shank

salt and pepper to taste

1 to 3 cloves of garlic

1 to 3 slices of fresh ginger

Rub the salt and pepper all over the leg of lamb. Cut the cloves of garlic and ginger slices in half. Plunge a paring knife into the leg at several places. Push a half-clove of garlic and half-slice of ginger deep into each slash. You may have to push your finger into the slashes to open them up first.

1 medium-size onion, sliced

1 to 3 sprigs of fresh rosemary

Scatter the onion and rosemary across the bottom of a roast pan. Put the seasoned leg of lamb on a roasting rack in the pan. Roast in the oven at 325° for 2 hours. You want the lamb not quite done. Remove the roast from the oven and cool.

Cut off the shank and place it on the seder plate. Remove the meat from the bone, but do not slice the meat yet. Drain the fat off of the drippings in the pan. Deglaze the pan by adding 2 to 3 cups of very hot beef, chicken, or mixed bullion. Stir and scrape the bottom of the pan to absorb all the drippings. Then pour this liquid into a bowl and set aside. If desired, some may be used to make gravy.

Set the two halves of the leg of lamb back in the pan. Before you sit down for your seder, pour some of the stock over the two halves of lamb in the pan and cover the roasting pan. Return the lamb to a 300° oven to rest during the first part of the ritual. It will finish roasting at this time. Then, as the table is being cleared for dinner, remove the lamb from the oven and slice. If desired, more hot stock may be poured over the slices, or a gravy may be made by thickening the stock with a flour paste or dissolved corn starch.

Fresh Brisket of Beef

If there are some family members or guests that are not lamb lovers, a small beef roast is also appropriate. Roast fresh brisket of beef is traditional at Passover. Beef was the meat of the Passover suppers of the priests that began on the 15th/16th of Nisan.

4 medium onions, peeled and sliced

2 whole carrots, peeled and sliced

2 stalks of celery, with leaves, sliced

12 peppercorns

3 bay leaves

2 cloves garlic

½-inch sliced fresh ginger

3 Tablespoons flour

1 teaspoon salt

¼ teaspoon pepper

1 teaspoon ground mustard

5 to 6 pounds of fresh beef brisket

Combine the sliced onions, carrots, celery, peppercorns, and bay leaves in the bottom of a roast pan. Stab the beef brisket in several places and insert the garlic and fresh ginger. Combine the flour, salt, ground pepper, and powdered mustard. Rub onto all sides of the beef brisket. Place the beef brisket on top of the vegetables in the roast pan. Sprinkle any remaining flour and seasoning on top.

Put the roast into a preheated 450° oven. After 10 minutes, drop the temperature to 350°. Roast at 350° for 3 to 3½ hours—that is, 30 to 35 minutes per pound. Turn the roast over once or twice during roasting. Add stock or wine if the vegetables become too dry, and baste the roast with the drippings.

Remove the beef brisket from the oven just before you sit down. Cover it with foil and let rest until you carve it for dinner.

Passover Rice Pilaf

Rice is not allowed at an Ashkenazic (European) Passover, but it is a staple of the Sephardic (Middle Eastern) seders.

2 cups white or brown rice

4 Tablespoons olive oil

1 whole leek, washed and chopped

1 clove garlic, pressed or finely chopped

½-inch fresh ginger, finely chopped

4 cups chicken stock, canned or bouillon

¼ to ½ teaspoon saffron, if desired

salt and pepper to taste

Heat the olive oil in a heavy metal pot. Stir in the rice and continue stirring while the rice cooks to a light brown.

Add the leeks, garlic, and fresh ginger. Stir until the leeks are glassy. Add the chicken stock and saffron. Taste for salt and pepper. Cover and set aside.

Just before you sit down for your seder, put the pot of Passover rice pilaf back on the fire and bring to a boil. Then place the pot in a 300° oven to cook until dinner.

"Remember...the leeks and the onions and the garlic (Num 11:5).

Sweet and Sour Red Beets, "A Red Sea"

6 cups cooked or canned beets, diced

½ cup white sugar

½ cup brown sugar

1 teaspoon salt

2 Tablespoons corn starch

5 whole cloves, ground or coarsely chopped

1 cup mild vinegar

grated rind and juice of 1 lemon

4 Tablespoons butter or margarine

Cook the sugar, salt, corn starch, cloves, lemon rind with
juice, and vinegar in heavy saucepan until the sauce is clear.
Add the diced beets and simmer for 30 minutes more. Put in
a casserole and place in warm oven or crockpot until dinner.
Stir in butter before you serve.

Passover Nicoise Salad,
"The Abundance of the Land and Its Produce"

The Passover nicoise salad can be a work of art. When the
seder plate is removed before dinner, the nicoise serves as a
beautiful replacement and as an hors d'oeuvres for the dinner. It also allows time for the slicing and serving of the
dinner by keeping the family and guests eating until the *piece
de la resistance* arrives.

Salad

> 8 new potatoes, cooked and diced, then
> marinated
>
> 2 jars gefilte fish, kosher for Passover (or one
> jar gefilte fish and one can tuna)
>
> 1 can whole string beans
>
> 1 can whole asparagus spears (or an equal
> amount of freshly steamed beans and
> asparagus)
>
> 1 sweet red onion, sliced, rings separated
>
> 1 red and/or yellow bell pepper, sliced thinly
> into circles
>
> 1 small can anchovy filets
>
> 24 small cherry tomatoes
>
> 6 hard-cooked eggs, peeled and sliced or
> quartered
>
> 1 small can pitted ripe olives
>
> 1 small can pitted green olives
>
> 1 large head Romaine lettuce

Salad Dressing

> 1 cup olive oil or salad oil
>
> 6 Tablespoons red wine vinegar

1 teaspoon salt

2 teaspoons dry mustard

1 Tablespoon prepared Dijon mustard

1 Tablespoon sugar

1 clove garlic, pressed or finely chopped

18 peppercorns

2 anchovy filets

Fresh tarragon or dried whole tarragon

Smash the peppercorns with the side of a chef's knife.

Put pepper, garlic, salt, sugar, mustard, anchovies and vinegar into a blender. Blend thoroughly. Add olive oil and mix thoroughly again. Add tarragon and mix slightly. Set aside until ready. Some of the dressing can be used to marinate the beans and asparagus and diced cooked potatoes.

Well before the seder, wash the Romaine, separate the leaves and pat them dry. Arrange the leaves on a very large platter so as to cover the entire surface. Drain the gefilte fish and/or tuna and place in the center of the tray. Place half the marinated potatoes in a pile on each end of the tray. Arrange the beans, asparagus and tomatoes on both sides of the gefilte fish and/or tuna to fill the space between the piles of marinated potatoes. Between these piles, place the pitted olives and quartered or sliced hard-cooked eggs. Scatter the sweet red onion and bell pepper rings over this magnificent production. Place an anchovy filet over each gefilte fish. Cover the whole creation loosely with plastic wrap and place it on the bottom shelf of your refrigerator until dinner.

Pour the salad dressing over all before serving. If desired, double the salad dressing recipe, especially for those wanting extra dressing served with your Passover Nicoise Salad masterpiece.

Set out small bowls of horseradish as well, as this is the traditional accompaniment of the gefilte fish.

Part II

HOW TO PREPARE AND PRESENT AN AUTHENTIC PASSOVER SEDER

At Church

Reserving the Space

Preparing for a Passover supper at your church or community center takes much planning and organization. The first order of business is setting a date and reserving that date on your church or community calendar. At Holy Family Church in San Jose, California, that means that the date must be submitted to the church staff for their meeting in early September to reserve places on the community calendar for the school year. Since Holy Family is an active community, a great many groups seek the use of the community center, meeting rooms, and youth center, as well as classrooms in the school for any number of important activities. If you underestimate the number of demands on the facilities, you may not find a place for you seder. It can happen, as it has happened at Holy Family.

Each church and community has its own timetable and number of spaces available for community gatherings such as a Passover supper. Make an appointment with those who are in charge of reservations as soon as possible and reserve your room or hall with the date officially set.

Planning the Seder Service and Dinner

Fortunately, our community at Holy Family Church has a well-established tradition of annual Passover seders, and the supreme authorities there are Blessie and Ernie La Scola and Fran and John Bermudes. This chapter is based upon their years of experience in planning and hosting these yearly events. All the suggestions, diagrams, checklists and recipes in this chapter are adapted from their original creations. I am simply shouting their virtues to the world; they deserve to be appreciated and loved far beyond the confines of our Silicon Valley home.

Planning a seder takes more work than planning a large dinner. The seder is a long ritual that takes from two-and-a-half to three hours, which must be taken into account. A host and hostess could simply lead the community as everyone follows in their Haggadahs, but the most effective seders are those in which parts and roles are given out to a number of others, especially young people. This takes some planning in advance.

Begin by forming the "Passover committees": the Food Committee, the Reservations Committee, the Kitchen Committee, and the Setup Committee. For a detailed description of each of these committees, see the sections devoted to them throughout the rest of this chapter.

Once you have your committees off and running, you can turn your attention to other details. The Materials and Supplies checklist on the next page will help you stay organized as you acquire each seder item.

Note that one of the suggested items under "Decorations for Tables" is a set of Star of David markers, one for each guest. (Not only do these markers assign places to the registered guests, they also can be used later as bookmarks!) Diagram 1 is a pattern for making these markers. Photocopying the pattern and cutting out the markers is a task you might want to delegate to a helper.

Another suggested item is the Haggadah, one for each person. If providing a Haggadah for every guest is not possible, try to provide at least one for every two guests to share. Someone should be delegated to photocopy enough copies of Part Three, the Haggadah Shel Pesach, for the community to use; however, make sure you get reproduction permission first (see the copyright page for where to write).

Next, using the Seder Service Assignment Sheet on page 38, start enlisting volunteers for the different parts of the seder. Fran Bermudes, a sixth-grade teacher at Holy Family in San Jose, usually handles this task. For the readings, she assigns some to her students. If she can't fill all the reading parts, she asks for volunteers from those who arrive early for the seder. For the hand-washing, once the tables and chairs are set up for the seder, she puts color dots on the backs of sixteen chairs, two in each hand-washing station. Later, she will invite the guests sitting in those chairs to help with the hand-washing.

Materials and Supplies for Seder Supper

Check off each of the following items as you acquire or arrange for it. The notes in parentheses indicate quantities necessary for a seder of more than one hundred people. If you have fewer guests, write in your quantities on the line provided.

☐ Tables (17 for 123 people) _____

☐ Covering for Tables (17) _____

☐ Decorations for Tables

    ☐ Name Tags (123) _____

    ☐ Star of David Markers (123) _____

    ☐ Blue Crepe for Center_____

☐ Candle Holders (2 each table = 34) ____

☐ Candles (2 each table = 34) _____

☐ Candles for Menorah (7) _____

☐ Matches (2 each table = 34) _____

☐ Color Dots Placed on Chairs to Mark Washing Stations (16) _____

☐ Salt (2 boxes) _____

☐ Small Cups for Salt Water (25) _____

☐ Banner _____

☐ Haggadahs (123) _____

For Washing Ceremonies

☐ Table_____

☐ Bowls for Washing Hands (8-10) _____

☐ Sliced Lemons (6-8) _____

☐ Hand Towels for 2 Washings (20) _____

☐ Elijah Cups (8) _____

☐ Purificators/Napkins (8)_____

Bread-Breaking Ceremony

☐ 2 Tables _____

☐ Small Baskets for Motzi-Matzah (8) ___

☐ Large Baskets for Sandwich (8) _____

☐ Flat Baskets for Afikoman (6-8) _____

Seder Ritual

☐ Plates with Dividers (123+)_____

☐ Small Cups for Wine/Juice (123+) _____

☐ Spoons (123+) _____

☐ Napkins (123+) _____

☐ Carafes for Juice (10) _____

☐ Seder Plate for Host _____

☐ Matzah Cover for Host _____

☐ Microphones

    ☐ For Host Table (1+) _____

    ☐ For Reading Parts (1)_____

☐ Prize for Finding Matzah

Dinner Service

☐ Tables for food, beverages, desserts _____

☐ Plates with Dividers (123+) _____

☐ Cups

    ☐ Wine (123+) _____

    ☐ Juice_____

    ☐ Coffee _____

☐ Silverware

    ☐ Knives (123+) _____

    ☐ Forks (123+) _____

    ☐ Spoons (123+)_____

    ☐ Napkins (123+)_____

Diagram 1: Star of David Markers

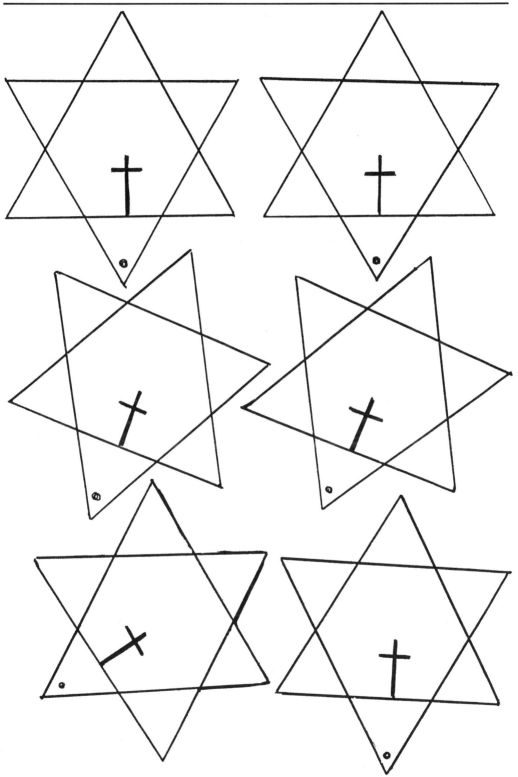

Seder Service Assignment Sheet

Readers for Lighting the Menorah

1. _____   4. _____

2. _____   5. _____

3. _____   6. _____

                              7. _____

Hand Washers

Bowls   Towels

1. _____   1. _____

2. _____   2. _____

3. _____   3. _____

4. _____   4. _____

5. _____   5. _____

6. _____   6. _____

7. _____   7. _____

8. _____   8. _____

Reading from John

Reader _____

Peter _____

Jesus _____

Page _____

The Four Questions

Youngest Child (English) _____   Youngest Child (Hebrew) _____

Children   Children

1. _____   1. _____

2. _____   2. _____

3. _____   3. _____

4. _____   4. _____

Servers to Bring the Baskets of Matzoth to the Tables

Motzi-Matzah

1. _____
2. _____
3. _____
4. _____
5. _____
6. _____
7. _____
8. _____

Hillel Sandwich

1. _____
2. _____
3. _____
4. _____
5. _____
6. _____
7. _____
8. _____

Servers for the Afikoman-Agape

Round Afikoman Loaves

1. _____
2. _____
3. _____
4. _____
5. _____
6. _____
7. _____
8. _____

Elijah Cups

1. _____
2. _____
3. _____
4. _____
5. _____
6. _____
7. _____
8. _____

Food and Reservations Committees

These two committees work closely together because you can't plan the quantity of food without knowing the number of people attending.

Food is obviously your biggest consideration. Ritual foods are sampled during the seder service; the complete dinner is served at the "Shulchan Orekh."

For the ritual foods, you may be lucky enough to have a professional cook in your community who is willing and able to shop for and prepare all of these foods in advance. If you do not have such a person, delegate the purchasing and preparing of the seder foods to the Food Committee:

☐ roast lamb pieces

☐ roast eggs

☐ horseradish

☐ Charoset

☐ parsley

☐ Matzah

☐ wine

☐ Afikoman

☐ plates and silverware

☐ table coverings and decorations

Give a copy of the Shopping List for Ritual Foods, page 42, to this committee. They can work from this checklist as they purchase each of the ingredients. Members of this committee will prepare the ritual foods at home, then bring their items to the church or the community center in plenty of time to have the tables set with them before the service.

For the seder dinner, even if your community is wealthy enough to hire a caterer, an old-fashioned pot-luck is the best dinner you can plan because it makes everyone an active participant. Again, this takes some planning and a capable Reservations Committee. As families and individuals make reservations to attend the community seder, the Reservations Committee keeps a record of what dish or casserole each family plans to bring so that you don't end up with too much of one food.

Your Reservations Committee must set a cut-off date for reservations or you will have people showing up at the last minute and there will be no food for them. The committee also needs to collect the money to cover the expenses of purchasing the ritual foods for the seder service and setting up the room or hall.

Shopping List for Ritual Foods

Refer to the recipes on the following pages to find out how much of each item to purchase. Write the necessary quantities on the lines provided; check the item off as it is acquired.

☐ Eggs _____ cartons

☐ Matzah _____ boxes

☐ Salt _____ boxes

☐ Wine _____ bottles

☐ Grape Juice _____ bottles

☐ Coffee _____ urns

☐ Punch _____ bottles

☐ Tea _____ urns

☐ Cream/Sugar _____ packets

☐ Lemons _____

☐ Parsley _____ bunches

☐ Lamb Shanks for seder plate _____

☐ Lamb for pieces on plates _____

Charoset

☐ Apples _____

☐ Celery _____ stalks

☐ Raisins _____ box(es)

☐ Walnuts/Almonds _____ pounds

☐ Honey _____ jar(s)

☐ Cinnamon _____

Horseradish or Maror

☐ Horseradish Root _____

☐ Whole Beets _____

☐ Sugar _____ box(es)

☐ White Wine Vinegar _____ bottle(s)

Communion Bread or Afikoman

☐ Whole Wheat Flour _____ bag(s)

☐ Oil _____ bottle(s)

☐ Honey _____

☐ Milk _____ carton(s)

☐ Baking Powder (Optional) ____ box(es)

Recipes for the Ritual Foods — "Serves One Hundred People"

- -

"Baytzah" or Roast Eggs

10 dozen eggs

Remove the eggs from their cartons. Eggs cannot be heated in their cartons because plastic cartons will shrink in the oven and paper cartons will insulate the eggs, leaving those in the middle not completely cooked.

Place the eggs in shallow pans and put them in a *cold* oven. Set the temperature to 200° and roast the eggs for 1½ hours. Turn the heat up to 300° and roast for at least thirty more minutes. At the end of 2 hours, check the eggs to see if the majority have brown spots on them, especially those in the middle. If most of the eggs are spotted, they are done. If not, cook another 30 minutes and check again.

When done, remove the eggs from the oven and cool. Return them to their cartons and refrigerate for several hours or over night. They must be thoroughly chilled before they are put on the plates for the seder.

One roasted egg will be placed upon each person's individual seder plate and a single egg on the host's seder plate.

- -

Lamb Morsels

1 leg of lamb (will be enough to supply pieces
for 100 to 150 people)

Roast at 300° for 2½ hours until done.

Let meat cool thoroughly. With a sharp knife cut the meat away from the bone. Then slice the meat into ¼" slices. Then cut each slice into individual pieces for the Hillel Sandwich. Each piece can then be pierced by toothpicks or bamboo skewers to form a cross. Put all of the pieces in a covered container and refrigerate.

One piece of this roast lamb will be placed in the center of each person's seder plates.

"Karpas" or Parsley

2 bunches of parsley

Wash thoroughly in plenty of water. Plunging the bunches into a pan full of water is best because the sand and dirt can fall to the bottom. Drain the parsley thoroughly and then separate the stems, breaking off those that are too long (longer than 3"). Place the separated stems in plastic bags and refrigerate.

One sprig of parsley will be placed on each person's seder plate and a small bunch of parsley on the host's seder plate.

Maror or Horseradish Puree

For the Brave and Adventuresome!

4 to 6 horseradish roots, or enough to make a gallon of puree

2 to 4 beets, whole, cooked, peeled

4 teaspoons salt

8 Tablespoons sugar

3 to 4 cups white wine vinegar

Wash the horseradish roots carefully by scrubbing them with a stiff brush. Cut off one of the tops for the host's seder plate and then peel the rest. Carefully cut the roots into large chunks.

Place no more than ¼ of the ingredients into a large food processor and grind into a puree. Add more liquid if needed.

Pour the puree into a large metal bowl with a secure cover. Continue the process with the remainder and add to the bowl. You will need at least 1 gallon of horseradish puree for 100 or more people.

One-half to one teaspoon of the horseradish puree will be put on each person's seder plate and the top of one of the roots on the host's seder plate.

For the Cautious and Sane

Buy enough bottles of horseradish—kosher for Passover—from the Passover display at your supermarket to equal one gallon of puree.

About one teaspoon of horseradish will be placed on each persons' seder plate and one small root on the host's seder plate.

Matzah or Unleavened Bread

5 boxes Matzah, kosher for Passover

Set 3 whole Matzah aside for the host's Matzah cover. Carefully break 10 Matzoth into at least 100 pieces, enough to allow everyone one piece. Divide these pieces among the eight small baskets for distribution at the Motzi-Matzah, the "Breaking of Bread."

Next, carefully break 20 Matzoth into at least 200 pieces, enough to allow everyone two pieces. Divide the 200 pieces among the 8 large baskets. Each person will receive two pieces of Matzoth in order to make their Hillel Sandwich at the conclusion of the first part of the ritual.

Wine, the Fruit of the Vine

1½ cases wine, kosher for Passover

Mogen David and *Maneschewitz* Concord Grape wines are traditional for Passover in the United States. *Carmel Wine* from Israel is now growing in popularity. These three produce a very sweet wine, kosher for Passover, for use at the seder, as this has been the custom for centuries. It seems that we Christians are responsible for this. Because there were periods when Christians denied Jews wine during the time of Passover, Jewish housewives began to hoard raisins during the year and as Passover approached they would make a bootleg raisin wine, which was naturally very sweet. From this practice grew the acquired taste for an especially sweet wine for use at the seder. I, too, prefer this sweet wine. Today, however, a number of dry wines, red and white, are also kosher for Passover. Therefore, the preference is yours.

Half the wine bottles will be placed on the tables for the first part of the service, two bottles on each table. Each person is required to drink 2 small glasses during the first half of the seder, then two more during the second half.

The 8 Elijah Cups will be filled near the conclusion of the ritual, at least at the same time as the fourth cup is poured.

8 large bottles grape juice

The amount of grape juice will be determined by the number
of children at your seder as well as the number of adults who
do not wish to drink wine. Since the four blessings are over
the "Fruit of the Vine," juice and wine are equally appropriate.

Over and above this amount of kosher wine and grape juice,
you will probably want to have a drier wine for the dinner
itself, along with coffee, tea, and punch.

- -

Blessie La Scola's Famous Charoset

This Charoset is a tradition at Holy Family parish.

> 12 to 15 apples, peeled and grated
>
> 9 to 12 stalks of celery, chopped very fine in
>   food processor
>
> 2 cups raisins, chopped together with walnuts
>   in food processor
>
> 1 cup walnuts, chopped together with raisins
>
> 2 to 3 cups kosher wine
>
> ¾ to 1 cup honey
>
> 3 Tablespoons cinnamon

Mix all ingredients in an extra large Tupperware bowl and
refrigerate. This Charoset tastes its best when made well in
advance! Blessie says that she prefers to make this marvelous
Charoset 5 to 10 days ahead. She says "It's great!" and I can
tell you "So say we all!"

At least one heaping tablespoon of the Charoset will be
placed on each person's seder plate and a generous portion
in a bowl upon the host's seder plate.

- -

Blessie La Scola's Afikoman, or Communion Bread

Blessie writes that this Afikoman recipe is the communion
bread recipe used at Holy Family "forever!"

> 2 cups whole wheat flour
>
> ⅓ cup oil
>
> ⅓ cup plus 1 Tablespoon honey
>
> ¾ to 1 cup milk

2 Tablespoons baking powder (optional)

Mix all the ingredients together in a large bowl and stir well. The baking powder may be used if the bread is for other than the liturgy or served at the Passover seder.

Grease 3 pie tins. Pour the batter into the center of the pie tins, dividing evenly. The batter will be thick and possibly lumpy.

Bake at 350° for about 15 to 20 minutes. Remove from oven and allow to cool for 10 minutes. Remove the bread from the pans and wrap in metal foil and refrigerate. One round loaf will easily serve 20 to 25 people.

At the Afikoman or Afikoman-Agape of the church or community seder, the whole round loaves will be passed around the tables and each person will break off a piece to eat.

Kitchen Committee

The Kitchen Committee supervises the pot-luck dinner. On the day of the seder service, their first task will be to set up the serving line of tables with napkins, plates, cups, silverware, and chaffing dishes, if used. Give them a copy of diagram 2, which illustrates a practical arrangement of tables for serving the dinner.

Set up two buffet tables (two tables each) to create four serving lines. Guests can file down both sides of each buffet. Place plates and silverware at the beginning of the line; follow these with salads, then hot foods.

Set up two other tables in proximity to the buffet lines. During dinner, these tables will hold the assorted drinks; toward the end of dinner, they will hold the assorted desserts.

After the tables are ready (the Setup Committee will be responsible for arranging the guests' tables), the Kitchen Committee can prepare to receive the potluck dishes. As guests bring the dishes, the committee members take the hot foods and store them in the warm oven, on hot-plates and in crock-pots; they take the cold foods and store them in the refrigerator.

When it's time for dinner, the Kitchen Committee will be in charge of serving. Four members remain in the kitchen and pass out food to the four "runners." The runners remove empty serving dishes from the buffet line and replace them with full ones. Two other committee members are responsible for the drink and dessert tables. During dinner, they ensure that there is plenty of coffee, tea, milk, punch, and juice for everyone; toward the end of dinner, they place the desserts on these tables as the runners clear the buffet line.

Diagram 2: Arrangement of Serving Tables

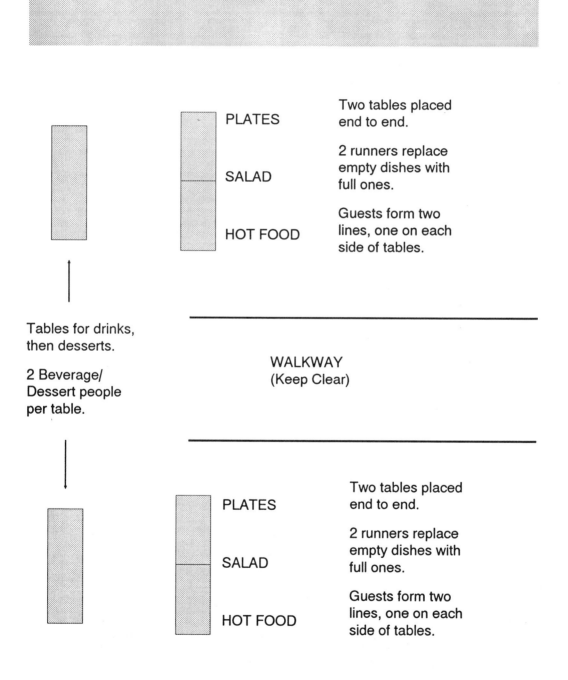

KITCHEN (4 PEOPLE)

Keep Counter Clear.

PLATES

Two tables placed
end to end.

SALAD

2 runners replace
empty dishes with
full ones.

HOT FOOD

Guests form two
lines, one on each
side of tables.

Tables for drinks,
then desserts.

2 Beverage/
Dessert people
per table.

WALKWAY
(Keep Clear)

PLATES

Two tables placed
end to end.

SALAD

2 runners replace
empty dishes with
full ones.

HOT FOOD

Guests form two
lines, one on each
side of tables.

Setup Committee

The Setup Committee is in charge of setting up the guest tables and placing the necessary items on these tables. Give them a copy of diagram 3, which illustrates a practical table arrangement, typical of the setup we use for our annual seder at Holy Family.

The Setup Committee should first arrange seventeen tables in the form of an "E." The back of the "E" is the head table, made up of three tables. Place chairs only on the outside of this head table. The three "legs" of the "E" stretch out from the head table, five tables at each end and four tables in the middle. Place chairs on both sides of these tables. Diagram 3 shows the exact placement of each table setting for 123 people; this may be used as a guide for chair placement as well.

Place two bottles of wine, kosher for Passover, on each table along with one decanter of grape juice.

Place two candle holders with candles on each table. Place a book of matches alongside each.

Place three small bowls of salt water on each table, in easy reach of everyone at that table for dipping their parsley sprigs into.

"E"-Shaped Table Arrangement

Diagram 3: "E"-Shaped Table Arrangement

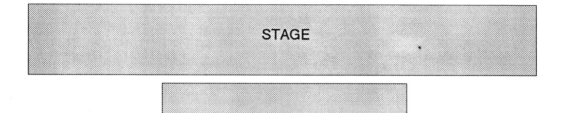

STAGE

15	13	11	9	7	5	3	1	2	4	6	8	10	12	14	16
17															18
19	20					21	22							23	24
25	26					27	28							29	30
31	32					33	34							35	36
37	38					39	40							41	42
43	44					45	46							47	48
49	50					51	52							53	54
55	56					57	58							59	60
61	62					63	64							65	66
67	68					69	70							71	72
73	74					75	76							77	78
79	80					81	82							83	84
85	86					87	88							89	90
91	92					93	94							95	96
97	98					99	100							101	102
103	104					105	106							107	108
109	110					111	112							113	114
115	116													117	118
119	120													121	123

BOWLS

Table with Menorah, Elijah Cups, and baskets

Place a single table just beyond the middle "leg" of the "E." Place eight bowls of water upon this table for use during the two washing of hands. Place two hand towels alongside each bowl, one to be used at the first washing of hands, the other for the second.

Set up one or two tables behind the head table and cover with white tablecloth(s). Place a seven-branched Menorah with candles in the center. In addition to the Menorah, place the following on this back table:

☐ 7-8 small baskets containing the pieces of Matzoth for the Motzi-Matzah

☐ 7-8 large baskets containing the pieces of Matzoth for the Hillel Sandwiches

☐ 7-8 flat baskets containing the sweet round loaves for the Afikoman-Agape

☐ 7-8 chalices to hold the wine for the Elijah Cups

Individual Seder Plates

Each of your guests must have his/her own seder plate. At every table setting, place a plate (preferably paper) and on it the following items (see diagram 4):

☐ a small piece of roast lamb, skewered to form a cross

☐ a roasted egg

☐ a generous tablespoon of Charoset

☐ a sprig of parsley

☐ a teaspoon of pureed horseradish

☐ a small pile of salt, to be used to salt the Matzah and roast egg

These items will be explained and eaten during the first part of the Passover ritual.

Diagram 4: Placement of Ritual Food on Seder Plate

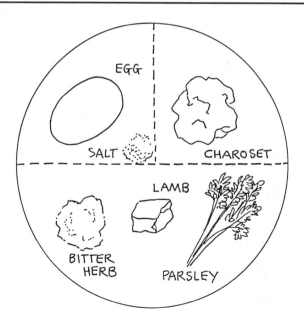

Readings for Lighting the Menorah, a Symbol of the Seven-Day Feast of Passover

Lighting the Menorah at the beginning of the seder ritual is a tradition at Holy Family. The custom was begun to remind students that Passover is a seven-day feast. If you choose to adopt this tradition, do these readings before starting the actual seder, which begins in the next part of this book.

The First Day

In the beginning
    there was darkness and silence.
God created the heavens and the earth.
God said,
    "Let there be light,"
and he called the light day;
    and the darkness he called night.

The Second Day

God made the sky.
In the sky he placed clouds to hold the moisture.
    And the sky was called heaven.

The Third Day

God gathered together the waters of the earth.
    He called them "seas."
And he named the dry land "earth."
On the land he made grow the grass and flowers
        and trees
    and each was the seed to replenish itself.

The Fourth Day

God made the sun to shine by day
    and the moon to shine by night.
The days, years, and the seasons were set by God.
Then he made the stars and placed them in the
        heavens.

The Fifth Day

God said, "Let the waters bring forth life,"
   and the seas and rivers became alive with whales
      and fish....
"Let there be birds" and the sky was filled with
   winged creatures....
"Be fruitful and multiply."

The Sixth Day

"Let the earth bring forth living creatures"
   and animals of all kinds filled the earth.
Then God created man and woman to have
   dominion over all of the earth.
They were the greatest of all God's creation.

The Seventh Day

On the seventh day
   God saw that all he had created was good!
And he rested on the seventh day.
We call this day "Sabbath" to give thanks to him
   who created us.

Part III

*HAGGADAH
SHEL PESACH*

THE PASSOVER
SEDER

The Order

לְהַדְלִיק נֵר שֶׁל יוֹם טוֹב
Ner Shel Yom Tov
Lighting the Holy Day Lights

1.
קַדֵּשׁ
Kaddesh
Sanctifying the Feast

2.
וּרְחַץ
Urechatz
Washing of Hands

3.
כַּרְפַּס
Karpas
Eating the Greens

4.
יַחַץ
Yachatz
Breaking the Middle Matzah

5.
מַגִּיד
Maggid
Narrating the Exodus

6.
רַחַץ
Rachatz
The Second Washing of Hands

7.
הַמּוֹצִיא
Ha-Motzi
The Breaking of Bread

of the Seder

8.

מַצָּה

Matzah

Reciting the Blessing

9.

מָרוֹר

Maror

Eating Bitter Herbs

10.

כּוֹרֵךְ

Korekh

Eating the Hillel Sandwich

11.

שֻׁלְחָן   עוֹרֵךְ

Shulchan Orekh

Dinner Is Served

12.

צָפוּן

Tzafun

Returning the Afikoman

13.

בָּרֵךְ

Barekh

Giving Thanks for the Meal

14.

הַלֵּל

Hallel

Reciting the Hallel

15.

נִרְצָה

Nirtzah

Conclusion of the Seder

לְהַדְלִיק נֵר שֶׁל יוֹם טוֹב
Ner Shel Yom Tov
Lighting the Holy Day Lights

The evening celebration begins with the lighting of the festival candles by the women present.

The mother, wife, sister or daughter closest to the candle lights it.

All mothers, wives, sisters and daughters recite the following blessing:

> We bless you O LORD our God,
> the king of the universe
> for you have sanctified us
> through the observance of your commandments
> and you have commanded us
> to light these holy day lights.[1]

בָּרוּךְ אַתָּה יְיָ אֱלֹהֵנוּ
מֶלֶךְ הָעוֹלָם
אֲשֶׁר קִדְּשָׁנוּ
בְּמִצְוֹתָיו
וְצִוָּנוּ
לְהַדְלִק נֵר
שֶׁל יוֹם טוֹב

All Fathers and Mothers:

> O LORD our God, bless our daughters as you blessed our spiritual mothers, Sarah and Rebecca, Rachel and Leah, and bless our sons as you blessed our spiritual fathers, Abraham and Isaac and Jacob, whom you blessed as Israel.

> May God bless you and keep all of you.
> May God be pleased with you and be gracious to you.
> May God watch over all of you and grant you His peace! (Priestly Prayer, Num 6:25-27).

The Meaning of Passover Observance

Father:

Welcome to our seder.

Tonight we are participating in history's most ancient and continuously observed festival. Tonight's ritual is called a "seder" because it follows a prescribed order in the unfolding of the service. The word "seder" means "order" in Hebrew. Throughout this ritual we will celebrate two principal events in the history of God's people. We will participate in the Exodus from Egypt, and we will recall that Jesus observed Passover with his disciples on the night before he died.

Mother:

Our table is set for a festive meal. In reality, however, our table setting becomes an environment in which the events of the Exodus from Egypt will be relived by all of us. We read in the Mishnah[2] (the written deposit of the Oral Torah) that in every generation each person should think of herself or himself as personally coming forth out of Egypt. That is what the bible means when it says in Exodus 13:8, "And you shall explain to your child on that day, saying, 'It is because of what the LORD did for *me* when I came out from Egypt'." Therefore, it was not only our ancestors whom the Holy One, blessed is He, redeemed from slavery, *we were also redeemed together with them* (Babylonian Talmud, Tractate, "Pesachim," 116b).

We are celebrating on this night, in unity with the whole people of God, the great Passover sacrifice. "And when your children ask what does this service mean to you, you will answer that this is the Passover offering of the LORD who passed over the houses of the children of Israel in Egypt, when He struck Egypt" (Ex 12:27).

Father:

At the conclusion of our seder, we will join together
in a simple Agape in memory of the fact that the Last
Supper was the Passover observance at the time of the
Temple. During the Passover supper, Jesus gathered
all of us to himself in the ritual sharing at the breaking
of bread (the Motzi-Matzah). After the supper, he
joined us to himself in the new covenant of his love.
Therefore, we will complete our evening, in unity
with the whole family of God, with a rededication of
ourselves to the new commandment of his Agape-
Love (Jn 13:34,35).

The Passover seder is also the celebration of the love,
compassion, and constant care that the Father of all
mercy has for all of his children. Four times during
the ritual, we are obligated to toast the LORD our
God for our liberation from bondage. These four cups
of the "Fruit of the Vine" are based upon the four
promises that the LORD made to the children of Israel
in Egypt through His servant, Moses:

וְהוֹצֵאתִ

"Wehotzeti"

"And I will bring you out from under the
tribulations of Egypt."

וְהִצַּלְתִּי

"Wehitzalti"

"And I will deliver you from their slavery."

וְגָאַלְתִּי

"Wega'alti"

"And I will redeem you with an arm outstretched
and with great judgments."

וְלָקַחְתִּי

"Welaqachti"

"And I will take you to Myself as My People."

וְהָיִיתִי

"Wehayiti"

"And I will be your God" (Ex 6:6,7).

Mother:

We read in the Mishnah that close to the hour of the evening sacrifice on the eve of Passover, a person must not eat anything until nightfall. Even the poorest in Israel must not eat anything until they are reclining at the Passover table. The hosts at each Passover supper should give to each person no less than four cups of wine. This is an obligation even if the food and drink must be supplied by money received from the charity plate (Babylonian Talmud, "Pesachim," Mishnah, 99b).[3]

At the time of the Second Temple, the wine was too strong or rough tasting to be drunk undiluted, since much of it was aged in pitch-lined animal hides. It was necessary to mix the wine with water to make it kosher for Passover. We read further in the Mishnah that these four cups must contain the standard mixture of water to wine, so that, as Rabbi Judah said, the mixture would still have the taste and appearance of wine. Furthermore, the rabbis taught that everyone was obligated to drink these four cups, including all of the women and children. Rabbi Judah is recorded to have rhetorically asked of what benefit is wine to women and children. It was decreed that they as well as the men were obligated to drink the four cups because women and children were also participants in that great miracle of the Exodus (Babylonian Talmud, "Pesachim," 108b).

1.

כַּדֵּשׁ

Kaddesh

Sanctifying the Feast

Everyone has a glass set before them at table. The glasses are filled with wine or grape juice. Father first blesses the "Fruit of the Vine" and then he blesses the festival.[4]

The first cup is called the Kiddush Cup (כּוֹס שֶׁל קָדֶשׁ), the Cup of Sanctification.

Father holds up his glass to recite the blessing of the "Fruit of the Vine":

> Blessed are you, O LORD our God,
>> the king of the universe
>> and creator of the Fruit of the Vine.

Father then recites the blessing for the festival:

> We praise you, O LORD our God,
>> the king of the universe,
> because you have chosen us
>> from among all the people of the earth,
> and you have exalted us
>> from among those of every spoken tongue,
> and you have sanctified us
>> through the observance of your commandments.

> Out of your love, you have given us seasons for gladness, holy festivals, and times for rejoicing.

> You have given us this holy feast of unleavened bread, which we celebrate each spring as this was the season of our deliverance. This is a sacred assembly that calls us together in a memorial of our coming forth from Egypt.

Because you have chosen us and blessed us from among all the people of the earth, we have inherited this holy festival to celebrate in gladness and in joy. Therefore, we bless you, O LORD. And you bless Israel (the people of God) and the festival seasons.

Father concludes the Kiddush with the ancient blessing for all festivals:

We bless you, O LORD our God,
   because you give to us our life.
You watch over us and you sustain us,
   and you have brought us to this holy season.[5]

Everyone lifts up their wine or juice glass and recites the blessing:

Blessed are you, O LORD our God,
   the king of the universe
   and creator of the Fruit of the Vine.

Everyone now drinks their wine or juice. The glass should be emptied, but remember, there are three more glasses required in the ritual.

2.

וּרְחַץ
Urechatz
Washing of Hands

Father and Mother now rise, pick up the bowls and towels, and assist everyone with the first washing of their hands. There is no blessing recited for this first washing. The commandment stipulates that the hands must be washed before touching any food.

This first washing of the hands is a reminder that at the time of the Second Temple the men, women and children had to immerse themselves completely in the ritual bath before they could participate in the Passover feast.

After assisting everyone with the washing of their hands, Father and Mother return to their places and resume the seder service.

Reflection on the Washing of Hands:
A Christian Addition

Since this would have been the time Jesus washed the disciples' feet, the following is included as a Christian addition to the traditional seder.

Reader:

Jesus, knowing that all things had been given to him by the Father, and that he had come forth from God and was now returning to God, rises from the supper and lays aside his outer garment, the Tallit. He takes a towel, and he girds it about himself. Then he pours water into a basin and he begins to wash the disciples' feet and to dry them with the towel which he has wrapped around him.

He then comes to Simon Peter who says to him, "Lord, are you going to wash my feet?" Jesus answers him, "What I am doing for you, you do not understand now, but you will understand me later.

Peter says to him, "You will not wash my feet—ever!"

Jesus answers him, "If I do not wash you, you have no place with me!"

Simon Peter says to him, "Lord, not only my feet but my hands and my head also."

Jesus says to him, "Having been bathed *(in the ritual bath)* there is no need but for the feet to be washed and you are all clean, but not all of you."

For he knew who would betray him and because of this he said, "Not all of you are clean." After he had washed their feet, he put on his outer garment and reclined again. He said to them,

Everyone:

"Do you understand what I have done for you?

You call me teacher and LORD, and you are correct, because I am.

If therefore I, the LORD and teacher, wash your feet—you also ought to wash one another's feet.

For I have given you an example: That as I did for you, you should do for each other.

As no slave is greater than his master, nor is a messenger greater than the one sending him.

If you understand these things, then you are blessed if you do them" (Jn 13:4-17).

3.

כַּרְפַּס

Karpas
Eating the Greens

This ceremony celebrates the arrival of spring as the season of our deliverance (Ex 13:4; "Abib," now pronounced "Aviv," means "spring").

The Karpas was the first course of the Passover supper at the time of the Second Temple. During this course, the roasted giblets of the paschal lambs were served on beds of leaf lettuce arranged upon large platters. It was the hors d'oeuvre before the main course of the meal. Pieces of lettuce were wrapped around the giblets and then they were dipped into bowls of saltwater or vinegar before they were eaten.

Today, parsley, watercress, celery or plain lettuce have replaced the giblets of Temple times. Everyone has a sprig of parsley on their plates. We will pick up these sprigs and dip them into the bowls of saltwater in the center of the tables. The saltwater represents the tears shed by the children of Israel while they were enslaved in Egypt.

Everyone says in unison:

Blessed are you, O LORD our God,
the king of the universe,
and the creator of the Fruit of the Earth.

Everyone dips their parsley sprigs into the salt water and eats them.

4.
יַחַץ
Yachatz
Breaking the Middle Matzah

One loaf of bread is served at the traditional Jewish meal. Two loaves, however, are served at the Sabbath supper on Friday evening as a reminder of the double portion of manna that was gathered each Friday by the Israelites in the wilderness (Ex 16:22). Because Passover is the preeminent feast of the Bible, three Matzot "loaves" are blessed and shared at the Passover supper.

The uppermost Matzah is named for the priest and is called "Kohen." The middle Matzah is named for the Levites and is called "Levi." The third Matzah is named for the people of God and is called "Yisrael."

These three "loaves" represent the three hereditary classes of the Jewish people at the time of the Second Temple. By everyone sharing them at the supper, they represent the unity of all the people at Passover.

Father removes the three Matzot from their protective cover and places then on a plate. He then breaks the middle Matzah in half, returns the two halves to the plate, and then up lifts the plate for all to see.

Father and Mother:

> Behold this, the bread of affliction that our
>   ancestors ate in the land of Egypt!
> Let all who are hungry come and eat with us,
>   let all who are needy come and share in our
>   Passover supper.
> Now we are here, next year may we be in the land
>   of Israel!
> Now we are slaves, next year may we all be free![6]

הָא לַחְמָא עַנְיָא דִּי אֲכָלוּ אַבְהָתָאַ
בְּאַרְעָא דְמִצְרָיִם.
כָּל דִּכְפִין יֵיתֵי וְיֵיכֹל / כָּל דִּצְרִיךְ יֵיתֵי וְיִפְסַח..
הָשַׁתָּא הָכָא / לְשָׁנָה הַבָּאָה בְּאַרְעָא דְיִשְׂרָאֵל .
הָשַׁתָּא עַבְדֵי / לְשָׁנָה הַבָּאָה בְּנֵי חוֹרִין .

It is the custom among many to turn on the porchlight at this point and leave the front door ajar for any unexpected guests. In the memory of past persecutions, others wait for the invitation of the prophet Elijah.

The Afikoman

The larger half of the broken Matzah is wrapped in a white napkin. This symbolizes the Israelites wrapping their unleavened dough in their bread troughs as they fled Egypt. This wrapped half of Matzah is reserved for the Afikoman to be eaten at the end of the meal. The seder ritual cannot be concluded without it. Father asks the children to cover their eyes while he hides it. The children, of course, will find the Afikoman and force Father to pay them something before they will give it back to him.

The smaller half of the broken Matzah will then be shared with the upper Matzah at the Ha-Motzi, which is the blessing of the bread that begins the formal meal.

The two other Matzot of the priest and the Levite are returned to their pockets in the Matzah cover.

The wine and juice glasses are now filled for the second time. This second cup is called the Cup of Narration (כּוֹס שֶׁל מַגִּד), Kos Shel Maggid.

The Afikoman:
A Christian Adaptation

The plate is returned to the table. Father wraps together both halves of middle Matzah in a white cloth and returns them to the Matzah cover or hides them in a safe place. Since the second Matzah could also represent the Son, the breaking, enshrouding, "burying," and then searching for it later could easily represent the death, burial, and resurrection of Jesus.

5.

מַגִּיד
Maggid
Narrating the Exodus

The lengthy recital of the events of the Exodus begins with the traditional Four Questions. These questions are traditionally asked by the youngest child present or by the youngest person at the seder table. The Four Questions are customarily sung in Hebrew.

אַרְבַּע הַקֻּשִׁיוֹת
The Four Questions

מַה נִשְׁתַּנָּה הַלַּיְלָה הַזֶּה מִכָּל־הַלֵּילוֹת?

Mah NeeshtahNAH HaLEIGHlah Hazay MeeCOAL HalayLOAT?

Why is this night different from all other nights?

1.   א. שֶׁבְּכָל הַלֵּילוֹת אָנוּ אוֹכְלִין חָמֵץ וּמַצָּה/ הַלַּיְלָה הַזֶּה כֻּלּוֹ מַצָּה.

ShehbuhKHOAL HalayLOAT Anoo OkhLEEN Chametz OO-Matzah.
HaLEIGHlah Hazeh Koolow Matzah.

On all other nights, we eat leavened or
    unleavened bread.
On this night we eat only unleavened bread.

2.   ב. שֶׁבְּכָל הַלֵּילוֹת אָנוּ אוֹכְלִין שְׁאָר יְרָקוֹת/ הַלַּיְלָה הַזֶּה מָרוֹר.

ShehbuKHOAL HalayLOAT Anoo OkhLEEN ShehARE YehrahKOAT.
HahLEIGHlah Hazeh MaROAR.

On all other nights we eat all kinds of herbs.
On this night we eat bitter herbs.

‎ג. שֶׁבְּכָל הַלֵּילוֹת אֵין אָנוּ מַטְבִּילִין אֲפִילוּ פַּעַם אֶחָת/ ‎.3
‎הַלַּילָה הַזֶּה שְׁתֵּי פְעָמִים.

*ShehbuKHOAL HalayLOAT Ayn Anoo MahtbeeLEEN
AhFEEloo PahAHM ehKHAT.
HahLEIGHlah Hazeh ShTAY FayahMEEM.*

On all other nights we don't dip even once.
On this night we dip twice.

‎ד. שֶׁבְּכָל הַלֵּילוֹת אָנוּ אוֹכְלִין בֵּין יוֹשְׁבִין וּבֵין מְסֻבִּין/ ‎.4
‎הַלַּילָה הַזֶּה כֻּלָּנוּ מְסֻבִּין.

*ShehbuKHOAL HalayLOAT Anoo OkhLEEN Bayn
YoshVEEN oo-Vayn MehsooBEEN.
HahLEIGHlah Hazeh KooLAHnoo Mehsoobeen.*

On all other nights we eat either seated or reclining.
On this night we eat reclining.[7]

**Father must now answer the young person's
questions:**

This night is very different from all other nights and
you are very wise to ask us the reason for that
difference. On this night, we will celebrate our
Exodus from Egypt. Notice the table before us! It is
especially set as the stage around which each one of
us will participate in reliving that momentous event.
Tonight, we will experience the flight from slavery to
freedom; how the Almighty changed our sorrow to
joy, and how the Holy One, Blessed is He, rescued
slaves groveling in misery within the house of
bondage and changed us through the observance of
His commandments into His own liberated people,
the people of God!

We eat only unleavened bread tonight because there was no time in our rush to freedom to allow our bread dough to rise.

> And the Egyptians pressured the people to hasten them while sending them away from their land; for they said, "All of us will be dead!" So the people took up their dough before it was leavened, binding their kneading troughs in their clothes and placing them upon their shoulders (Ex 12:33).

Mother:

We eat especially Bitter Herbs tonight to taste again the bitterness of slavery. As we read in the Torah,

> Egypt made the children of Israel to slave oppressively by making their lives *bitter* with hard work fashioning clay bricks and with all kinds of work in the field (Ex 1:13).

We dip our food twice this evening, once into saltwater to recall the tears shed in cruel slavery and bitter bondage, and we dip the harsh-tasting horseradish into the sweet Charoset to remind us to keep our faith in God, because He changes our cries of sorrow into shouts of joy.

Father:

We recline about the table this evening to recall that while the Holy Temple stood in Jerusalem, everyone reclined on couches at the Passover supper to express their joy of being set free on this night. As we read in Scripture,

> You shall tell your child, We were slaves to the Pharaoh in Egypt, but the LORD brought us out of Egypt with a powerful hand and by an outstretched arm" (Dt 6:21; 26:8).

If the Holy One, Blessed is He, had not brought our ancestors out of Egypt, then we and our children and our children's children would still be slaves to a Pharaoh in Egypt. Therefore, if we possessed all wisdom, and all understanding, and we were endowed with the wisdom of great age, and had complete understanding of the Sacred Scriptures, it would still be commanded of us to recount the events of our departure from Egypt. And whoever recalls the most details about our Exodus from Egypt is the most worthy of all our praise!

Mother:

An example of the meritorious discussion of the Exodus event is contained in the traditional Haggadah. It concerns some famous second-century rabbis at the school in Bene Berak, near ancient Jaffa. They were laboriously involved in writing down all of the previously memorized Oral Torah and the Oral Traditions of Temple times. Their completed written work became the Mishnah, the oldest part of the Talmud.

On this occasion, the learned rabbis were so engrossed in their analysis of the Exodus event that they lost all sense of time.

Father:

It happened at that time that Rabbi Eliezer, Rabbi Joshua, Rabbi Elazar ben Azariah, Rabbi Akiba and Rabbi Tarfon, as they were reclining about the seder table at Bene Berak while discussing the events of the Exodus from Egypt, they did not notice that they had been engaged in their deliberation all night long. Finally, their disciples came to them and said, "Our Masters, it is now time to recite the Morning Shema!"

Mother:

Rabbi Jose, the Galilean, said: "Since you say that the Egyptians in Egypt were beaten with Ten Plagues, then at the Red Sea they were stricken with fifty plagues! Why? What does it say (in the Bible) about the Egyptians? And the magicians said to Pharaoh, 'It is the *finger* of God' (Ex 8:15). But at the Red Sea, what does it say? 'And Israel saw the *Great Hand* with which the LORD acted against Egypt. The people were fearful of the LORD, and they had confidence in the LORD and Moses his servant' (Ex 14:31). By how much were they stricken by one finger? With Ten Plagues! Therefore, if it can be said that they were beaten by Ten Plagues in Egypt, then it follows that they were struck by fifty plagues at the Sea!"

Everyone:

Rabbi Elazar ben Azariah said, "Look, I am nearly seventy years of age and I could not recall why the Exodus from Egypt was discussed at night. Then Ben Zoma interpreted the verse in Scripture, 'As it is said, So that you may remember the day you came out of the land of Egypt *all the days of your life*' (Dt 16:3). '*Days of your life*,' he said, 'would mean only the days, but *all of the days of your life* means the nights as well!' Other Wise Men have said, '*days of your life*' means in this age only, but '*all of the days of your life*' means in the Messianic Age as well."

Father:

Blessed is our Omnipresent God, Blessed is He who gave the Covenant to His People Israel, Blessed is He!

Four times we read in Scripture that parents are commanded to explain the Passover ritual to their children:

> When your children shall say to you "what does this ritual mean to you" (Ex 12:26).

And you shall explain to you child on that day,
saying, "This is because of what the LORD did
for me when I came out from Egypt" (Ex 13:8).

When your child asks you, hereafter, "what does
all this mean?" (Ex 13:14).

And when your child asks you in the future,
"What are the testimonies, regulations, and laws
that the LORD has commanded you to obey?"
(Dt 6:20).

Mother:

From these verses, it is understood that the bible
speaks to us about four different children: the Child
who is Wise, the Rebellious Child, the
Unsophisticated Child, and the Child who is too
young to ask questions.

Father:

The Wise Child is attentive and asks, "What are the
testimonies, regulations, and laws the LORD has
commanded you to obey?" (Dt 6:20). You must
instruct these children in the ancient customs and
rules governing the observance of Passover. Introduce
them into the ritual whereby we celebrate these
obligations that are placed upon us. Especially the
commitment that there is to be no eating nor
involvement in any revelry after the Afikoman
(Babylonian Talmud, "Pesachim," 119b).

The Rebellious Child says, "What does this ritual
mean to you?" (Ex 12:26). Not feeling a part of the
celebration, that child asks "to you" as an outsider
having no place in the observance. That child should
be answered, "This is because of what the LORD did
for *me* when *I* came out from Egypt" (Ex 13:8). "For
me" because I have accepted God's call to redemption,
but that child would have remained a slave in Egypt
by rebelling against God's actions in saving His
people.

Mother:

The Unsophisticated Child asks, "What does all this mean?" and you will explain to that child, "By the might of his hand, the LORD brought us out of Egypt, out from the house of slavery" (Ex 13:14).

For the Child too young to ask why this evening is so different from all others, that child should be introduced to the story of the Exodus by interpreting the unusual items on the seder table and explaining in understandable language, "This is because of what the LORD did for *me* when *I* came out of Egypt" (Ex 13:8).

Everyone:

We read in the Mishnah that it is the duty of parents to instruct their children according to their intelligence. Parents are to begin the narration by explaining the shame experienced in slavery at the beginning and conclude the instructions by praising God for the deliverance of His people from oppression.

Father:

In the beginning, our ancestors worshiped idols, but our Omnipresent God called us to serve Him, as it says in Torah:

And Joshua said to all the People, "Thus speaks the LORD (YHWH), the GOD of Israel, In the past, Terah the father of Abraham and the father of Nahor, your ancestors, lived beyond the river (Euphrates) and they served other gods. But I took your father Abraham from beyond the River and led him throughout all of the Land of Canaan. I multiplied his seed and give Isaac to him. To Isaac I gave Jacob and Esau. I gave the mountain region of Seir to Esau as his possession, but Jacob and his family went down into Egypt" (Jos 24:2-4).

Mother:

We bless the LORD who keeps His promise to Israel. For the Holy One, blessed is He, calculated the time He had allotted until He would fulfill His promise to our father Abraham, a promise He had made to him in the covenant cut between the animals' two halves (Gen 15:7-12). As we read,

> And He said to Abram: "You must know for certain that your descendants will become aliens in a land that is not theirs, and they will be enslaved and afflicted there for four hundred years. But, I will bring judgment against the nation that enslaves them and thereafter they will go out from it with great wealth" (Gen 15:13,14).

Everyone lifts up their glasses and says:

This promise made by God to our father Abraham was cherished by our ancestors, and it has sustained us as well. Because not just one person has risen up to destroy us, but in every succeeding generation another has appeared and attempted to exterminate us. But the Holy One, blessed is He, has always delivered us from out of their hands.

Everyone returns their glasses to the table.

Midrash on Deuteronomy 26:5[8]

Father:

It is wise to ask what the Aramean (Syrian) Laban intended to do to our ancestor, Jacob. While Pharaoh decreed that all newborn male infants should be killed, Laban wanted to exterminate Jacob and his whole family.

As we read in Scripture,

An Aramean would have destroyed my father, but he went down to Egypt to live there with only a few people. And he became a nation there that was great and mighty and numerous (Dt 26:5)[9]

"He went down to Egypt" — Compelled by the will of God! (Gen 15:13,14).

"And he lived there" — Scripture teaches us that our ancestor Jacob did not go down into Egypt to settle, but only to sojourn there:

> And they said to Pharaoh, "We have come to sojourn in the land, because there is no grazing ground for your servants' flocks, as the famine is heavy in the land of Canaan. Now, please let your servants live in the land of Goshen" (Gen 47:4).

"Only a few people" — As it says,

> "Your ancestors went down to Egypt, just seventy people. But now the LORD (YHWH) your God has made you as numerous as the stars in the heavens" (Dt 10:22).

"He became a nation there" — We learn from this that Israel became a distinguishable group there (Ex 1:8,9).

"Great and mighty" — As it says in Scripture,

> And the children of Israel were fruitful and teeming and numerous, and became very, very strong. The land was filled with them (Ex 1:7).

"and numerous" — As it says,

> I have caused you to multiply like the shoots of the field. And you did multiply and become great and you became precious jewels. Your breasts have formed and your hair has grown, yet you are naked and bare (Ez 16:7).[10]

עֶשֶׂר מַכּוֹת
The Ten Plagues

Father:

These are the Ten Plagues with which God punished the Egyptians with ever-increasing intensity.

Everyone:

These are the Ten Plagues that fell upon the Egyptians because of their Pharaoh's stubborn arrogance!

Mother:

But all people are the children of our God. Even when they intend to destroy us, we cannot rejoice in their suffering. In the true spirit of the Haggadah, we must not rejoice in the suffering of others.

"Is there not One Father of us all? Has not the One God created all of us? Why, then do we betray our brothers and sisters and thereby profane the Covenant of our Ancestors" (Mal 2:10).

The Egyptian people were severely punished because of their Pharaoh's hard-hearted refusal to release the Israelites from their bondage to him. But we cannot rejoice in their suffering, "Are you not like the children of the Ethiopians to me, O children of Israel?" Therefore, our second glass of wine cannot be full as we remember their torment. Instead, we will remove some of the wine or juice from our glasses.

Father:

So that our second cup, the Cup of the Exodus Narration, will not remain full, we will remove some of the "Fruit of the Vine." With a spoon or our little finger we will take some of the contents of our glasses and drop it onto our plates as we name each one of the Ten Plagues:

Blood, "Dam" דָם

Frogs, "Tzefardea" צְפַרְדֵּעַ

Lice, "Kinnim" כִּנִּים

Wild Beasts, "Awerove" עָרוֹב

Cattle Disease, "Dayver" דֶּבֶר

Boils "Shicheen" שְׁחִין

Hail "Barahd" בָּרָד

Locusts, "Arbeh" אַרְבֶּה

Darkness, "Choshekh" חֹשֶׁךְ

Death of Their Firstborn, "Makat Bekhorot"
מַכַּת בְּכֹרוֹת

Everyone:

We grieve over the horrors suffered by our fellow human beings so that we could be liberated. And yet, we can thank and we do praise our Lord and God for our redemption.

Everyone lifts their glasses and recites together:

And she, the Shekhinah [the cloud of fire and divine presence; Ex 13:21-22; 14:19-20], protected our forbearers and us. Not one enemy alone has risen up to destroy us, but rather, in every generation there have arisen individuals and groups intent upon annihilating us. But the Holy One, blessed is He, delivers us from their evil plans.[11]

Everyone sets their glasses down on the table.

Mother:

The mood of the narration suddenly changes at this point from the dwelling upon misery and suffering in

Egypt to the joy and happiness expressed by a free people living in their own land. The bridge to the next section is the delightful song, the "Dayyenu."

Father:

The Dayyenu has fifteen short verses that end with the one word chorus, "Dayyenu!" It is a Hebrew word that may be loosely translated as, "That alone would have been enough for us!" The fifteen verses are said to represent the number of steps from the Court of the Women in the Temple to the inner Court of the Priests. The Levites stood upon these steps during the Passover sacrifice and repeatedly sang the Hallel. "Hallel" is the Hebrew name for the collection of The Great Psalms of Praise (Ps 113-118; 136). "Halleluyah" means, "Let us sing The Great Psalms of Praise to YAH (YHWH)!"

Mother:

The Dayyenu also expresses the joy of the millions of pilgrims who ascended to Jerusalem each year for the feast of Passover while the Temple stood. There they actively participated in the Passover sacrifice in the Holy Temple. They came dressed in white because they all were elevated to the status of the priesthood for the pilgrimage feast of Passover ("Chag Ha-Pesach"), and were therefore required to wear the white linen robes and turbans of the clergy (Ex 39:27). As a memorial of the Passover sacrifice and universal priesthood of the people in Temple times, the tradition continues to this day of the men wearing white "Kipot" ("Yarmulkes") at the seder. Moreover, in observant Jewish homes, Father as Host wears a white garment as he leads his family in the Passover ritual.

Father:

Let us joyfully ascend to Jerusalem as well to participate in our memorial of the Passover sacrifice. That unique sacrifice was offered in the Holy Temple by Israelites[12] who had traveled from the ends of the known world to participate in this great paschal offering as "one people" (עַם אֶחָד). We will also participate in the paschal supper that was shared by all in the holy city of Jerusalem as a "single family" (מִשְׁפָּחָה אַחַת) by our sampling the symbolic foods of Temple times.

דַּיֵּנוּ
Dayyenu[13]

Everyone:

How many great blessings has the omnipresent Lord bestowed upon us?

Mother and Father:

If only He had brought us out of Egypt,
And not brought judgments upon them!

Everyone:

Dayyenu!

Mother and Father:

If only He had brought judgments upon them
And not defeated their gods!

Everyone:

Dayyenu!

Mother and Father:

If only He had defeated their gods,
And not slain their firstborn!

Everyone:

Dayyenu!

Mother and Father:

If only He had slain their firstborn,
And not given us their wealth!

Everyone:

Dayyenu!

Mother and Father:

If only He had given us their wealth,
And not divided the sea for us!

Everyone:

Dayyenu!

Mother and Father:

If only He had divided the sea for us,
And not made our way through the midst of it on dry
    land!

Everyone:

Dayyenu!

Mother and Father:

If only He had made our passage on dry land,
And not drowned our oppressors in the depths of the
    sea!

Everyone:

Dayyenu!

Mother and Father:

If only He had left our oppressors in the depths of the
    sea,
And not taken good care of us for forty years!

Everyone:

Dayyenu!

Mother and Father:

If only He had watched over us for forty years,
And not fed us with manna!

Everyone:

Dayyenu!

Mother and Father:

If only He had fed us with manna,
And not given to us the Sabbath!

Everyone:

Dayyenu!

Mother and Father:

If only He had given us the Sabbath,
And not brought us before the face of Mount Sinai!

Everyone:

Dayyenu!

Mother and Father:

If only He had brought us before Mount Sinai,
And not given the Torah to us!

Everyone:

Dayyenu!

Mother and Father:

If only He had given us Torah,
And not brought us into the Land of Israel!

Everyone:

Dayyenu!

Mother and Father:

If only He had brought us into the Land of Israel,
And not built for us His Holy Temple!

Everyone:

Dayyenu!

How much more then, in doubled and redoubled measure, has the Omnipresent One a claim upon our gratitude!

He brought us out of Egypt, and brought judgment upon them and upon their gods. He slew their firstborn and gave us their wealth! He divided the sea for us and led us through it on dry ground.

He plunged our oppressors into the depths of the sea!

He took care of us in the wilderness for forty years and He fed us with manna! He gave us the Sabbath for rest and He brought us before Mount Sinai, and He gave us the Torah!

He brought us into the Land of Israel and built for us His Holy Temple where we could atone for all our sins!

Mother:

The Passover supper of Temple times was the sacred banquet that completed the Passover sacrifice. Men, women, and children were all elevated to the dignity of the priesthood in order to participate. Therefore they came under the Levitical law of purification that required them to bathe in the ritual bath and put on white linen robes (Babylonian Talmud, "Pesachim," 109a,b). They then were privileged to eat the entire paschal lamb (Ex 12:8-10), not just the laity's portion (Lv 7:33-36). They all participated in the whole

Passover sacrifice, as well, because they all shared in the eating of the roasted flesh of the paschal offering that was the main course of the Passover supper.[14]

Father:

While the Temple stood, the great Rabbi Gamaliel used to say that whoever does not explain these three essential items at the Passover supper does not fulfill his paschal obligations (Babylonian Talmud, "Pesachim," Mishnah 116a,b).

And these three things are:

The Passover Sacrifice, "Pesach" פֶּסַח

The Unleavened Bread, "Matzah" מַצָּה

The Bitter Herbs, "Maror" מָרוֹר

Mother:

By emphasizing the equality of these three items, the rabbis were able to continue the observance of Passover without the sacrifice of the paschal lambs in the Temple and without the annual pilgrimage to Jerusalem where the paschal supper was eaten. By showing the unity of the one-day feast of Passover (Josephus, *Antiquities* [248]) with the seven-day Feast of Unleavened Bread (Josephus, *Antiquities* [249]), the unleavened bread was able to take the place of the paschal lamb as the sacrificial object to be shared in the seder supper.[15]

Everyone:

The roasted flesh of the Passover sacrifice that our ancestors ate at the time of the Temple, why was there the obligation to eat it?

Father:[16]

Because the Holy One, Blessed is He, *passed over* the houses of our ancestors in Egypt. As we read in Torah,

It is the Passover sacrifice of the LORD (YHWH)
Who passed over the houses of the children of
Israel in Egypt, when He struck Egypt and
spared our houses. And the people bowed and
worshiped, and the children of Israel went out
and did as the LORD (YHWH) had commanded
Moses and Aaron (Ex 12:27,28).

Everyone:

This Matzah our ancestors ate, and which we eat on
this night, what is the meaning of it?

Mother:

The women were required to make the unleavened
bread very quickly because the dough our ancestors
made had no time to rise when the King of kings
revealed Himself to them and Redeemed them. As we
read,

And they baked the dough which they had
brought out from Egypt into plain unleavened
wafers, for it was not leavened; because they
were driven out of Egypt and had no time to
delay in order to prepare food for the journey
(Ex 12:39).

Everyone:

These bitter herbs that our ancestors ate, and that we
eat on this night, what is the reason for eating it?

Father and Mother:

Because the Egyptians made the lives of our ancestors
bitter in slavery and, therefore, we must taste the
same harshness as we share their bitter experience. As
we read,

And they made their lives bitter with hard work
in clay and in the fashioning of bricks and with
all kinds of work in the field. In all the work they

forced them to do, they pressured them with harshness! (Ex 1:14)

Father:

As we all share these three obligatory foods tonight, we are not simply remembering what happened so very long ago, we are actually participating in all of those events. This Passover ritual is called a "Zikaron" in Hebrew (Ex 12:14), an "Anamnesis" in Greek (1 Cor 11:24,25), and a "Memoriam" in Latin. The seder is a re-actualization of the Exodus. That means that by means of this Passover ritual we are not only bringing all of the events of the Exodus into the present so that we can also experience them, *it means that we actually become participants in all of events of the Exodus.*

Mother:

An undisputed commandment of the Oral Law from the time of the Temple is preserved in the Mishnah, and it says that *from generation to generation, each person is bound to regard himself or herself as personally coming forth out of Egypt.* As it says in the Torah,

> and you shall tell your child on that day that this is because of what the LORD (YHWH) did for me when I came out from Egypt" (Ex 13:8; Babylonian Talmud, "Pesachim" 116b).

Everyone lifts up their glasses and recites:

Therefore, it is our duty to thank, praise, laud, glorify, exalt, honor, bless, extol, and adore Him Who wrought all of these miracles for our ancestors and for ourselves.

He brought all of us forth from bondage into freedom, from sorrow into joy, from mourning into festivity, from darkness into great light, and from slavery into redemption.

Therefore, let us say before Him —
"Halleluyah!" (Babylonian Talmud, "Pesachim,"
116b).

The Hallel

The Hallel (Ps 113-118; 136) was chanted by the Levites
in the Temple as the paschal lambs were sacrificed
there. The Hallel was also sung by the people before and
after eating their Passover supper. Psalms 113 and 114
were sung before the main course; Psalms 115 through
118 and Psalm 136 were sung after the blessing for the
food. That was an obligation because it was a sacrificial
meal. The Passover supper of Temple times was the
conclusion of the Passover sacrifice. The Passover sacrifice was both a peace offering and communion sacrifice.

Everyone:

Halleluyah!

Praise Him, you servants of the LORD!
   Praise the name of the LORD (YHWH)!

The name of the LORD (YHWH) is praised from
   now and forever.
From the rising of the sun to its going down
   the name of the LORD (YHWH) is praised.

The LORD (YHWH) is high above all the nations,
   His glory above the heavens.

Who is like the LORD (YHWH) our God?
Who sits enthroned on high
   and who looks down upon the heavens and the
      earth.

He raises the poor up from the dust
   and the needy from the dunghill
to sit them among the aristocracy
   among the nobles of their own people

He causes the childless woman
to joyfully dwell in her house with her children.

Halleluyah!

Psalm 114

Everyone:

When Israel came out of Egypt,
the house of Jacob, from a people speaking an
alien tongue,

Mother and Father:

Judah became his sanctuary,
Israel his dominion.
The sea saw this and fled;
the Jordan river turned back!

Everyone:

The mountains skipped like rams,
the hills like lambs of the flock!

Mother and Father:

Sea, what is it that you flee?
Jordan, what is it that turns you back?
You mountains, why do you skip like rams?
You hills, like the lambs of the flock?

Everyone:

Before the face of the LORD
the earth trembles,
before the face of the God of Jacob!
Who turned the rock into a pool of water
and the flinty stone into a gushing spring.

Everyone lifts up their glasses and recites:

Blessed are you, O LORD our God,
    the king of the universe,
our Redeemer and the Redeemer of our forbearers
    in Egypt,
who brought us to this night on which we eat
    unleavened bread and bitter herbs.
Therefore, O LORD our God and the God of our
    ancestors,
bring us to other festivals and holy days that come
    to us in peace,
joyful in the rebuilding of Your holy city and
    joyous in Your service.
There we shall eat of the sacrifices and paschal
    offerings whose blood will be worthily poured
    out upon the sides of your altar.[17]

Everyone recites the blessing and drinks the second glass of the "Fruit of the Vine":

Blessed are you, O LORD our God,
    the king of the universe,
    and creator of the Fruit of the Vine.

6.
רָחַץ
Rachatz
The Second Washing of Hands

Mother:

We will now prepare to eat a little bit of the ritual food of Temple times. First, we must wash our hands for the second time before the Matzah is blessed and shared.

Mother and Father rise for the second time and, taking the bowls of water and towels, they assist everyone with the washing of their hands.

Everyone:

Blessed are you, O LORD our God,
the king of the universe,
You have sanctified us through the observance of
Your commandments,
and commanded us concerning the washing of our
hands.

7.

הַמּוֹצִיא

Ha-Motzi

The Breaking of Bread

After he returns to his place at the table, the Host of the
seder, Father, just as was done at the time of the Temple,
removes the top Matzah—the priests' loaf—from its
safe place in the Matzah cover and recites the double
blessing over it. The Matzah is first blessed as bread
with the recital of the "Ha-Motzi," the traditional blessing of the bread said at the beginning of every Sabbath
and holy day meal. Then the Matzah is blessed with its
own blessing stating the requirement of eating only
unleavened bread throughout the seven or eight days
of Passover.[18]

**Father, removing the upper Matzah from the
Matzah cover, recites:**

Blessed are you, O LORD our God,
   the king of the universe
   who brings forth bread from the earth.

בָּרוּךְ אַתָּה/ יְיָ אֱלֹהֵינוּ/ מֶלֶךְ הָעוֹלָם/ הַמּוֹצִיא לֶחֶם מִן הָאָרֶץ .

8.

מַצָּה
Matzah
Reciting the Blessing

Then, breaking the Matzah so that there is a piece for everyone, Father says:

Blessed are you, O LORD our God,
  the king of the universe,
You have sanctified us through the observance of
  Your commandments
and commanded us concerning the eating of this
  Matzah.

בָּרוּךְ אַתָּה/ יְיָ אֱלֹהֵינוּ/ מֶלֶךְ הָעֹלָם/
אֲשֶׁר קִדְּשָׁנוּ בְּמִצְוֹתָיו וְצִוָּנוּ עַל אֲכִילַת מַצָּה.

מוֹצִיא מַצָּה
Motzi-Matzah

Mother:

When everyone has received their piece of Matzah,
take some of the salt on your plate and sprinkle it
onto the Matzah. This reminds us of the sacramental
nature of the Passover Matzah. It is salted just as the
paschal lambs were salted as a sacrificial offering
before roasting them over hot coals for the feast.
Now, everyone will repeat the double blessing and
eat the Passover Matzah.

Everyone:

Blessed are you, O LORD our God,
  the king of the universe,
  who brings forth bread from the earth.

Blessed are you, O LORD our God,
   the king of the universe,
You have sanctified us through the observance of
   Your commandments
and commanded us concerning the eating of the
   Passover Matzah.

9.
מָרוֹר
Maror
Eating the Bitter Herbs

Father:

> We are now commanded to eat the bitter herbs.
> Because it is horseradish, this must be done carefully.
> With your spoon, take a very small portion of the
> Maror from your plate onto the spoon and then take
> twice as much of the Charoset onto the spoon as
> well—to cut the stinging effect that the horseradish
> has. When ready, we all will recite the appropriate
> blessing and eat the bitter herb.

Everyone:

> Blessed are you, O LORD our God,
>   the king of the universe,
> You have sanctified us through the observance of
>   Your commandments,
> and commanded us concerning the eating of the
>   bitter herbs.

10.
כּוֹרֵךְ
Korekh
Eating the Hillel Sandwich

Mother:

We will conclude our eating of a symbolic meal of Temple times by making the "Hillel Sandwich."

Father:

To the question put by a potential convert to Judaism, could Hillel recite the whole Torah while he was standing on one foot, the great sage responded by doing so while admonishing the young man, "Whatsoever is hateful to you, do not do to another! That is the whole Torah. All the rest is commentary!"

The Talmud records that Hillel used to wrap lamb and bitter herbs together in a soft Matzah. To Hillel, the commandment to eat the Passover lamb together with unleavened bread and bitter herbs (Ex 12:8) was an important obligation. Having a great understanding of the meaning of the Passover ritual, he realized that slavery and freedom were to be experienced together at the supper of the Passover sacrifice. The bread of affliction displayed at the invitation to Passover ("Ha-Lachma") was also the bread of freedom shared at the breaking of bread ("Ha-Motzi"). The Passover commentary teaches us that it is the obligation of free people to be ever mindful of those who are still bound in any kind of physical servitude, emotional bondage or political oppression. And all those still oppressed must never forget that our God is the God of liberation and of the liberators!

Mother:

Father will now remove the Matzah of the people, "Yisrael," from the Matzah cover. He will break it and divide it into enough pieces so that there are two pieces for everyone. Each one of us will make the Hillel Sandwich from them (Babylonian Talmud, "Pesachim," 115a).

Father:

Everyone take one of the pieces of the Matzah. Then place some of the bitter herb on it, along with some of the Charoset. Then close your Hillel Sandwich with the second piece of Matzah. Now let us all say together:

Everyone:

Blessed are you, O LORD our God,
    the king of the universe,
You have sanctified us through the observance of
    Your commandments
and commanded us to eat the paschal lamb
    together with unleavened bread and bitter herbs
    (Ex 12:8).

Everyone eats their Hillel Sandwich.

The Hillel Sandwich:
A Christian Adaptation

Father:

The Passover Sacrifices ended when the Romans
destroyed the Holy Temple; as a consequence, Jews
can no longer eat the paschal lamb at their Passover
suppers. The seder was then adapted by the rabbis in
order to center the meal around the eating of
unleavened bread as a substitute for the lamb eaten
during Temple times. This was possible because the
one-day feast of Passover had already become the
first day of the seven-day feast of unleavened bread
(Mk 14:1,12).

Mother:

But the Gospel of John (Jn 1:29,36) and the epistles of
Paul (1 Cor 5:7) and Peter (1 Pt 1:19) saw in Jesus'
death the final and perfect Passover sacrifice, which
atones for all of our sins (Heb 9:11-28). In the second
century, Melito of Sardis gave a Passover homily in
which he explained how Christ had replaced the
sacrifice of the Passover lambs in the Temple with his
offering of himself. Justin Martyr continued the theme
in his "Dialogue with Trypho." He considered the
commandment to roast the whole lamb at Passover to
be a symbol of Christ's death on the cross because the
two wooden spits that transfixed the paschal sacrifice
and held it over the fire actually formed a cross.
Therefore, lamb holds a prominent place in a
Christian seder.

Father removes the Matzah of the people, "Yisrael,"
from the Matzah cover. He breaks it, dividing it into
enough pieces so that there are two pieces for everyone.
Each one makes the Hillel Sandwich from these.

Father:

Everyone take one of the pieces of the Matzah. Then
place some of the bitter herb on it, along with some of
the Charoset. Then, removing the skewers from the
piece of lamb, place the lamb morsel on the
horseradish and Charoset. Close your Hillel
Sandwich with the second piece of Matzah. Now let
us all say together:

Everyone:

Blessed are you, O LORD our God,
    the king of the universe,
You have sanctified us through the observance of
    Your commandments
and commanded us to eat lamb with unleavened
    bread and bitter herbs (Ex 12:8).

Everyone eats their Hillel Sandwich.

בֵּצָה

Baytzah
Eating the Roasted Egg:
A Christian Addition

Mother:

Eating the Hillel Sandwich concludes the first part of
the ritual of the Passover seder. However, there
remains one more symbolic item on our seder plate.
That is the roasted egg, called the "Baytzah." In
Jewish homes, the roasted egg is eaten without any
ceremony after it is dipped into salt water. It
represents mourning for the loss of the Holy Temple
and its sacrifices. But over the centuries Christians
have taken this lowly egg and turned it into a joyous
symbol of the resurrection.

Father:

After the destruction of the Temple by the Romans in
70 C.E. (A.D.) and the abolition of the Passover
sacrifice there, paschal lambs could no longer be eaten
by Jews at Passover. The rabbinical seder was created
to enable the continuation of the Passover observance
without the sacrificed lamb. The paschal lamb was
replaced by the unleavened bread as the focal point of
the service.

Mother:

But the Passover sacrifice and the Holy Temple were
not forgotten. Upon the great platters that had once
held the whole roasted paschal lambs during the
Passover supper of Temple times, families now
placed a roasted lamb bone in memory of the
sacrificed Passover lamb and a roasted egg as a
symbol of their mourning for the loss of the Temple.
A hard-cooked egg had long been a token of

mourning and an example of strength in adversity, because the longer it cooks the harder it gets.

Father:

The first Jewish Christians followed the same customs as their Jewish neighbors and relatives, because they mourned the loss of the Holy Temple as well. They soon realized, however, that Christians still had the ultimate Passover sacrifice, Jesus. As St. Paul wrote,

> Christ was sacrificed for us as our Passover! So that we should celebrate the feast, not with old leaven or the leaven of malice and wickedness, but with the unleavened bread of sincerity and truth! (1 Cor 5:7,8)

Mother:

Moreover, Christians were not bereft of the Temple as their Jewish kin were. As St. Paul also wrote,

> Do you not know that you are God's temple and the Spirit of God dwells within you? If anyone defile the temple of God, God will bring that person to ruin; because the temple of God is Holy, and that is what you are! (1 Cor 3:16,17)

Father:

Consequently, very early in the church, the Jewish emblem of mourning became the Christian symbol of the resurrection. The early Christians reasoned that just as the stony shell cannot contain the living chick within it and breaks when it hatches, the stone of the tomb could not restrain Christ when he rose from the dead.

Mother:

The custom arose in the Eastern church of smashing colored, hard-cooked eggs at Easter, while shouting, "Christ is risen," and then responding, "He is risen, indeed!"

Father:

To help us connect our Passover observance (פֶּסַח ,
"Pesach") with Easter, we must recognize that
"Pascha" (in Greek, Πασχα) was the original name
for Easter. That much we know from history, but
what is not generally known is that the Greek word
"Pascha" is actually the same word written in Greek
letters as the Aramaic word for Passover, which is
also (פַּסְחָא) or "Pascha!"

Let us all pick up our roasted egg and smash it onto
our plates as we make our Easter and paschal
proclamation.

Mother and Father:

Christ is risen!

Everyone smashes their eggs on their plate and responds:

He is risen indeed!

11.
שֻׁלְחָן עוֹרֵךְ
Shulchan Orekh
Dinner Is Served

The seder plate is now removed, and the table cleared for the dinner that has been prepared. The Passover ritual will conclude after dinner.

12.

צָפוּן

Tzafun

Returning the Afikoman

After dinner, the table is cleared of everything except the wine or juice glasses, the plate with the Matzah cover, the Elijah Cup, and the burning candles.

Father and Mother invite everyone to recover their Haggadahs for use during the remainder of the seder service. If he still has it, Father places the Afikoman (the "hidden" Matzah) on a plate before him and uncovers it for all to see.

If, however, the Afikoman has been spirited away and hidden somewhere by the children, Father must find out who has it and offer that child some reward for its return.

Since the Afikoman is the last thing to be eaten at the seder, the ritual cannot continue until the Afikoman is returned. Once returned, Father resumes the seder.[19]

13.

בָּרֵךְ

Barekh

Giving Thanks for the Meal

Everyone's glasses are filled for the third time. In Hebrew, this third cup is called the Cup of Blessing (כּוֹס שֶׁל בְּרָכָה), or more familiarly, the Eucharistic Cup (1 Cor 10:16).

Father:

Let us say the blessing for our food, my honored friends.

Everyone:

The name of the Lord is praised from this time forth and forever!

Father and Mother:

Praised be our God of whose bounty we have partaken and through whose goodness we all live.

Everyone:

Praised is He and praised is His holy name.

Father:

Blessed are you, O LORD our God,
    the king of the Universe,
Who, in Your goodness, sustain the whole world
    with love, kindness, and compassion.
You provide food (bread) for all flesh (BaSaR),
    for your mercy endures forever (Ps 136:25).

Because of your great love,
  we have not lacked sustenance and may we
  never lack provisions for Your great name's sake.
You, O God, take care of all, do good to all, and
  provide food for all your creatures whom You
    have created.
Praised be You, O LORD, who provides food for all.

Mother:

We thank You, O LORD our God,
  for the good, pleasant and spacious land which
    You have given to us as an inheritance from our
    ancestors,
  for having liberated us from the land of Egypt,
    and redeemed us from the house of slavery.
We thank You for your covenant that You have
    sealed in our flesh,
  for Your Torah which You have taught us, and
    for your Commandments which You have made
    known to us.
We also thank You for the gift of life which You,
    in Your love and kindness, have bestowed upon
    us,
  and for the food with which You nourish and
    sustain us continually, in every season, every
    day, and even every hour.

Everyone:

For all these blessings, O LORD our God,
  we give you thanks and we praise you.
May your holy name be praised by every living
  creature continually and forever,
  as we are told in the Torah,
    "and you shall eat and be satisfied, and you shall
    bless the LORD your God in the good land
    which He has given to you" (Dt 8:10).
We praise you, O LORD, for the land and its
  produce.

Father:

Have compassion, O LORD our God,
    for Your People Israel,
    for Jerusalem Your City,
    for Zion the abode of Your Glory,
    for the Royal House of David, Your Anointed,
   and upon the great and Holy Temple called by
     your Name.
Our God and our Father,
  take care of and nourish us,
  sustain and maintain us, and
  speedily bring an end to all of our sorrows.

Everyone:

Our God and the God of our ancestors,
    on this festival of unleavened bread,
  be ever mindful of us and of our forbearers.
Hasten the age of the Messiah, the Son of David.
Remember Jerusalem your Holy City,
   and all your people,
   the House of Israel,
  who are blessed by your deliverance, love,
    kindness, mercy, life and peace!

Remember us on this day, O LORD our God,
  to bless us with life and well-being.
With your promise of deliverance and mercy,
  spare us and be gracious to us,
  have compassion on us and save us.

We look to you, our God,
  for you are a gracious and merciful king.

Father:

May the Merciful Father bless us and all who are
   dear to us,
  even as our fathers, Abraham, Isaac and Jacob
   were blessed,
   each with his own complete blessing;
May He bless each and everyone of us,
  each of us with our own perfect blessing.

And to this let us all say...

Everyone:

Amen!

Everyone lifts up their glasses and recites:

Blessed are you, O LORD our God,
   the king of the universe,
   and creator of the fruit of the vine!

Everyone drinks their third glass, the Cup of Blessing, which was known to Greek-speaking Jews as the Eucharistic Cup.

14.

הַלֵּל

Hallel

Reciting the Hallel

All glasses are filled with the "Fruit of the Vine" for the fourth time. This fourth cup is called the Cup of the Hallel (כּוֹס שֶׁל הַלֵּל), "Kos Shel Hallel." At this time Father will also fill the Elijah Cup (כּוֹס שֶׁל אֵלִיָּהוּ), "Kos Shel Eliyahu." For many, it is customary at this time to open the door and turn on the porchlight as an invitation to the Prophet Elijah to join the family at the seder table.

Mother:

> There is a universal belief that the prophet Elijah will appear at Passover and announce the arrival of the Messiah. That is why we open the door and pour a special cup of wine for him. Many believe that he enters every home at seder, and while not seen, he sips from the cup set out for him. Young children notice that after a little while there is less wine in his cup, especially if Father has drawn a line at the original level, and they are certain that Elijah did join them briefly.

Father:

> The prophet Elijah is expected to explain the difficult sections of the Bible and to settle all disputes. He is predicted to bring peace and love to every family: "Behold, I am sending you the Prophet Elijah before the coming of the great and fearful Day of the LORD (YHWH), and he will turn the hearts of their parents to their children and the hearts of the children to their parents" (Mal 3:24). Let us greet the prophet with the ancient salutation offered to honored guests:

Everyone:

Blessed is he who comes!
(בָּרוּךְ הַבָּה) BaRUKH HaBAH!

Father and Mother:

Elijah, the Prophet,
Elijah, the Tishbite,
Elijah, the Gileadite!

Come speedily and bring
the Messiah, the Son of David!

Everyone:

Elijah, the Prophet,
Elijah, the Tishbite,
Elijah, the Gileadite!

Come speedily and bring
the Messiah, the Son of David!

הַלְלוּיָה
Halleluyah[20]

Psalm 115

Father:

Not to us, O LORD (YHWH), not to us,
but to your Name give glory,
because of your Love and your Truth.

Everyone:

Why do the Gentile nations say:
where is their God?

Mother:

Our God is in the Heavens
    Finding pleasure in all that He has made.

Everyone:

Their idols are of silver and gold
    they are the works of human hands.

They have mouths but do not speak
    eyes that do not see
    ears that do not hear
    a nose but cannot smell.

Their hands cannot feel,
    their feet cannot walk;
no utterance is heard in their throats.

Father:

Those who make them are like them,
    Everyone who has faith in them!

Mother:

O Israel,
    Have faith in the LORD (YHWH);
He is your helper and your shield.

O House of Aaron,
    Have faith in the LORD;
He is your helper and your shield.

All you who revere the LORD
    Trust in the LORD;
He is your helper and your shield.

Everyone:

The LORD is ever mindful of us;
  He will bless us,
  He will bless the house of Israel,
  He will bless the house of Aaron,
  He will bless all those who revere him
    from the least to the greatest.

Father:

He will add to you
  Add to you and your children.

Everyone:

Blessed are you O LORD (YHWH)
  who made the heavens and the earth.

The heaven of heavens belong to the LORD
    (YHWH)
  but the earth He has given to the children of
    Adam.
The dead do not praise the LORD
  nor those who go down into the grave
but we will bless the LORD
  from now and forever!

Halleluyah!

Psalm 116

Father:

I love,
  because the LORD (YHWH) hears my voice
    and my prayers.

Mother:

He inclined His ears to me.
  Throughout my day
    I will call upon Him.

Everyone:

But the cord of death encircled me
  and the boundaries of the grave overtook me.
I find myself in anguish and in grief.

Father:

I call upon the Name of the LORD (YHWH)
  I beseech You, O LORD (YHWH)
    Save my life!

Mother:

The LORD (YHWH) is compassionate and just.
Our God is merciful;
  the LORD (YHWH) protects the defenseless.

Everyone:

I was low
  but the LORD (YHWH) saved me.
Return O my life to your resting place
  because the LORD (YHWH) has rewarded you!

Father:

Having pulled my life out of death,
  my eyes away from tears,
  and my feet from stumbling.

Mother:

I will walk before the LORD (YHWH)
  in the land of the Living.
I have believed, therefore I speak!

Everyone:

Before I was greatly afflicted
  and I said in my alarm, "Everyone is a liar."

Father and Mother:

> What shall I return to the LORD (YHWH)
>> for all that He has bestowed upon me?
> I will lift up the Cup of Salvation
>> and I will call upon the Name of the LORD
>> (YHWH)!

Everyone:

> Please now will I pay my vows to the LORD
>> (YHWH)
>> in the presence of all of His people!

Mother and Father:

> Costly is the death of His faithful ones
>> in the eyes of the LORD (YHWH).
> I pray, O LORD (YHWH), that I am truly your
>> servant.
> I am your servant and the Child of your
>> Maidservant
>> and You have loosened my bonds.

Everyone:

> I will sacrifice to you the sacrifice of thanksgiving
>> and I will call upon the name of the LORD
>> (YHWH)
> I will pay my vows, please now! To the LORD
>> (YHWH)
>> in the presence of all of his people
>> in the courts of the house of the LORD (YHWH)
>> in the midst of you, O Jerusalem!

> Halleluyah!

Psalm 117

Mother and Father:

Praise the LORD (YHWH) all you nations!
  Praise Him all you peoples!

Everyone:

Because He is mighty over us
  and the truth and the love of the LORD (YHWH)
    are forever!

Halleluyah!

Psalm 118

Father and Mother:

Give thanks to the LORD (YHWH), for He is good,
  His Love for us is forever!

Everyone:

Let the house of Aaron say,
  that his love for us is forever!

Let the God-fearing say,
  that His love for us is forever!

Father:

Out of my distress I called upon the LORD
    (YHWH)
  And He answered me and set me free!

Mother:

The Lord is with me,
  I will not be afraid.
What can anyone do to me?

Father:

The LORD is with me as my helper,
  I shall see the downfall of my enemies.

Mother:

It is better to rely on the LORD
  Than to depend upon any person.

Everyone:

It is better to rely upon the LORD
  than to depend upon princes.

Many nations encircled me;
  in the name of the LORD I overcame them!

They circled all about me;
  in the name of the LORD I overcame them!

They swarmed about me like bees;
  they were consumed as a fire among thorns
because in the name of the LORD I overcame them!

Father:

They thrust at me to make me fall;
  but the LORD (YHWH) came to my assistance.
The LORD (YHWH) is my strength and my song,
  and He has become my Deliverer.

Listen! The joyous song of victory
  is heard in the tents of the Righteous;

The might of the LORD (YHWH) is triumphant!
The power of the LORD (YHWH) is exalted!
The strength of the LORD (YHWH) is victorious!

Mother:

I shall not die, but will live
  to recount the works of the LORD.

The LORD has severely chastened me
  but He has not given me over to death.

Open to me the Gates of Righteousness
   that I may enter and praise the LORD.

This is the Gate of the LORD,
   the Righteous alone shall enter here!

(By ancient tradition, each of the following verses is repeated:)

Father and Mother:

I thank You, O LORD,
   that You have answered me,
   and have become my Deliverer.
The stone that the builders rejected,
   has become the cornerstone!
This is the work of the LORD,
   and it is marvelous in our eyes!

Everyone:

I thank you, O LORD (YHWH),
   that you have answered me,
   and have become my deliverer.
The stone that the builders rejected,
   has become the cornerstone!
This is the work of the LORD (YHWH),
   and it is marvelous in our eyes!

Father and Mother:

This is the day which the LORD (YHWH) has
      made;
   Let us rejoice and be glad in it.

I beseech You, LORD (YHWH),
   salvation please now ("Hoshiah Na"[21])!
I beseech You, LORD (YHWH), success please now!

Blessed is He who comes in the Name of the LORD.
   We bless Him from the House of the LORD!

Everyone:

This is the day which the LORD has made;
   let us rejoice and be glad in it!

I beseech you, LORD (YHWH),
   salvation please now ("Hoshiah Na")!
I beseech you, LORD (YHWH), success please now!

Blessed is He who comes in the Name of the LORD.
   We bless Him from the House of the LORD!

Father and Mother:

God is LORD (YHWH) and He has given us light;
   join the festival procession with woven branches
      up to the horns of the Altar (singing),
   "You are my God and I thank You!"
   "You are my God and I extol You!"

Everyone:

God is LORD and He has given us light;
   join the festival procession with woven branches
      up to the horns of the altar (singing),
   "You are my God and I thank you!"
   "You are my God and I extol you!"

Father and Mother:

Give thanks to the LORD for He is good,
   because His love is everlasting!

Everyone:

Give thanks to the LORD for He is good,
   because His love is everlasting!

Prayer Concluding the Hallel

Everyone:

All your works praise you, O LORD our God,
    and your faithful ones,
        the just who do your will,
    together with all your people,
        the house of Israel,
    shall praise you in joyous song.

We shall thank, exalt, revere and sanctify you,
    and ascribe sovereignty to your holy name,
        O our king!

For it is good to give you thanks and it is fitting to
        sing praises to your holy name,
    for you are God from everlasting unto
        everlasting!

15.

נִרְצָה

Nirtzah
Conclusion of the Seder

Everyone:

Blessed are you, O LORD our God,
   the king of the universe.
We praise you for the vine
   and the fruit of the vine
   and for the produce of the field,
     for the broad, good and beautiful land
     that you were pleased to bestow
     upon our ancestors and upon us
     that we may eat from its fruitfulness
     and be satisfied by its goodness!
Please now!
Be compassionate with your people, Israel,
   over your city, Jerusalem,
   over Zion, the place of your glory,
   and over your sanctuary.

We rejoice on this day
    the feast of unleavened bread
   because you are good
    O LORD,
   and the benefactor to all.
We thank you for the land
   and for the fruit of the vine.

Blessed are you O LORD
   for the land
   and for the fruit of the vine!

Mother and Father:

Now our seder is concluded,
   every law and custom fulfilled;

as we have gathered here to celebrate this Passover
tonight
may we be able to gather again for seder next year.

O pure one who dwells on high!
Raise up the countless assembled congregations of
your people,
and speedily lead the offshoots of your stock,
now redeemed,
to holy Zion with song!

Everyone:

Blessed are you, O LORD our God,
the king of the universe
and creator of the Fruit of the Vine.

Everyone drinks the Cup of the Hallel, then exclaims:

Next year in Jerusalem!

Notes

1. This prayer over the festival lights is ancient. It does not mention candles because at the time of Christ oil lamps were used. Oil lamps were lit by mothers and wives before all sabbaths and festivals, especially the Passover supper. Oil lamps at the time of the Second Temple were constructed to hold enough oil to burn from sunset to sunset. Jesus' mother said this prayer over the oil lamps in her home on all the sabbaths and holidays of her life and may very well have led the other women in this prayer before the Last Supper.

2. At the time of Christ, the bible or Torah was believed to have two parts. One was the Written Bible, but of equal importance was the Oral Teachings of the great sages. The Oral Teachings were not written down but were memorized by the disciples of the rabbis. There was a special class of disciple that was adept at memorizing. Called "Tanna'im," a Tanna was an authority on the Oral Torah and the Oral Teaching of the religious authorities. Only after the destruction of the Jewish nation by the Romans in 66-73 AD did the rabbis collect the memorized Oral Teaching in writing to preserve it.

3. Throughout history, Jewish communities have taken up collections to insure that every family has enough to eat and drink at Passover so that their seders are joyful. It is from that same sense of responsibility for the needs of others that we continue that tradition with our charitable collections of food and toys for the poor at Thanksgiving and Christmas.

4. Jesus certainly recited these two blessings at the Last Supper, since both are discussed in the Mishnah. Luke states that Jesus took the first cup at the beginning of the supper and blessed it by reciting the Kiddush, and then he said, "Take this and divide it among you" (Lk 22:17). Sharing the Kiddush Cup had special meaning at the time of the Second Temple. Because very great crowds assembled in Jerusalem at Passover, many families had to join together as a single group for the celebration. Yet Exodus 12:3 states the Passover lamb must be eaten by families, so using Exodus 12:4 as a rationale, several families were joined together as one family by sharing the one Kiddush Cup.

5. This blessing, called the "Shehecheyannu," was not said at the Last Supper. At the time of the Second Temple, this prayer was said by a priest over the firstborn son of a family when the child was "purchased back from the LORD" by his parents with a simple sacrifice in the Temple. The ceremony was called "pidyon haben" (Lk 2:22-24). After the Temple was destroyed and the Passover sacrifice could no longer be offered there, the rabbis decreed that the blood shed by the firstborn at his circumcision (the "B'rith Milah" or the "circumcision covenant") was a suitable substitution for the atoning blood of the Passover lambs shed during Temple times for the sanctification of the feast. The redeeming prayer over the firstborn was then added to the Passover supper ritual to

express this later sanctification. Subsequently, the Shehecheyanu was added to the Kiddush on the first day of all the festivals.

6. This prayer is usually recited in Aramaic instead of Hebrew. Aramaic is the language acquired by the Jews during their Babylonian captivity. Scholars are fairly unanimous in believing that this prayer originated in Babylon as well because the prayer suggests that the people are still enslaved and are exiled from the land of Israel. Even in Aramaic, which was the everyday language that Jesus spoke, there are several Hebrew names, such as "Mitzrayim" (Egypt), "Pesach" (Passover) and "Yisrael" (Israel).

7. This fourth question was not asked at the Last Supper. Instead the children asked, "On all other nights we eat meat roasted, stewed or boiled. On this night we eat only roasted meat." After the destruction of the Temple, no paschal lambs could be eaten at Passover, and then the question about boiled or roast meat was replaced by this one about reclining.

8. The traditional Haggadah is the source of this ancient Midrash on Deuteronomy 26:5.

9. The first line of Deuteronomy 26:5 should read "My father was a wandering Aramean." For the sake of this Midrash, however, the vowels of the Hebrew word,"oBeD" are changed to "iBeD," which means "would have destroyed." Scholars believe that this is a disguised reference to the Syrian king Antiochus IV Epiphanes, who intended to abolish Judaism.

10. Israel was youthful but still immature in Egypt. Maturity came with Israel's acceptance of the Covenant (Torah) at Mount Sinai. Deuteronomy 26:5-10 was a profession of faith made on the feast of Pentecost (Dt 26:1-11). At the Pentecost (Shavuoth) profession, the first line reads, "My father was a wandering Aramean." Many traditional Haggadahs contain a Midrash of all of Deuteronomy 26:5-10.

11. Karen G. R. Roekard, *The Santa Cruz Haggadah* (Capitola, California: Hineni Consciousness Press, 1991), 29.

12. "An Israelite killed the paschal lamb and the priest caught the animal's blood in a basin." Was a layman permitted to sacrifice? The Tanna informs us that was indeed the case! It is lawful that the ritual slaughter of the Passover sacrifice be done by a lay Israelite. "And the priest caught the blood" informs us that it became the obligation of the priest, from the time he received the blood in a basin until the blood was "sprinkled" against the sides of the altar (Babylonian Talmud, "Pesachim," 64b).

13. This song, or one very much like it, was sung at the Last Supper. It was and is very popular. Historians noted that since the refrains end with a reference to the Temple, the song existed at Second Temple times, if not long before.

14. Baruch M. Bokser, *Origins of the Seder*, Berkeley: University of California Press, 1984. It is recorded in the Mishnah that Rabbi Judah ben Bathyra taught that while the Second Temple existed, the rejoicing at the Passover supper must be centered upon the eating of the roasted flesh of the paschal lamb. The Hebrew word for "flesh" is "BaSar" and means "body," "flesh," "flesh of the sacrifice," and "living creature" or "person." The Aramaic word is almost identical, "BiSRA," and means exactly the same thing. Our Lord's words at the Last Supper were "DeN BiSReY": "This, My Body."

15. Josephus explained in *Antiquities of the Jews* that the feast of Passover was celebrated on the 14th of the Hebrew month Nisan (III, 10, 5.[248]) and the Feast of Unleavened Bread began on the 15th (III, 10, 5.[249]). Although all the people had to remain in Jerusalem throughout the 14th and 15th, they could leave on the 16th. If the Sabbath fell on the 15th or 16th, however, then the people could not leave until the 17th. The Priests and Levites, on the other hand, had the obligation of observing all seven of the succeeding days in the Temple, "for it is intended as a feast for the priest(s) on every one of those days."

16. Father reads this because the laymen did the actual sacrifice of the lambs in the Temple.

17. This blessing was added to the first part of the Hallel by the second-century Rabbi Akiba.

18. These two blessings were said by Jesus at the Last Supper. The Gospels state that during the meal Jesus took bread, blessed and broke it and gave it to his disciples (Mk 14:22). By their calling the Matzah "bread," they identify that this was at the Motzi-Matzah of the Passover supper, wherein the unleavened bread is first blessed as bread and then as Matzah. It is then broken and shared with everyone. The breaking and sharing of bread had great meaning for the Jews; called the Ha-Motzi, it signified that the sharing of bread and the meal united everyone in a special covenant relationship. Naturally, the original name for the Eucharist was "Ha-Motzi," the "Breaking of Bread" (Acts 2:42).

19. The Afikoman is traditionally eaten at this point. A Christian adaptation of the ritual reserves the Afikoman for the Agape observed after the conclusion of the seder.

20. Psalms 115, 116, and 117 may be omitted. For a shorter service turn to page 119.

21. The original meaning of "Hosanna," "Hoshiah Na," is "Salvation Please Now!" and not "Hurray." The crowds of people were not cheering Jesus upon his entry into Jerusalem; they were imploring him to liberate them from the cruel Romans.

Part IV

AGAPE

A CHRISTIAN
CONCLUSION
TO THE SEDER

Father:

We will conclude our evening with a Christian
adaptation of the Afikoman. In the Jewish home, the
Afikoman is eaten just before the thanksgiving grace
after the supper is recited. At the time of the Temple,
when the paschal lambs were still sacrificed in the
Temple and the roasted flesh eaten at the Passover
suppers throughout the Holy City, the Afikoman was
a piece of the sacrificed lamb "about the size of an
olive" eaten in a formal Hillel Sandwich. That final
morsel of the paschal lamb was combined with
Matzah and Maror (Ex 12:8) and was eaten just before
the prayer of affirmation was recited at the Nirtzah,
concluding the Passover ritual. That ritual
consumption of the flesh of the paschal lamb, while
stating that all customs and laws had been fulfilled,
was an affirmation that all paschal obligations had
been met.

Mother:

Jesus gathered all of us to himself at the
Motzi-Matzah, the breaking of bread, of that last
Passover supper. In our respectful recognition of the
Eucharist which he bequeathed to us, we will share
the Afikoman of our seder in a simple ceremony
expressing our Agape-Love.

Father:

In this simple Agape, we will also share the Elijah
Cup. The Elijah Cup may be called the fifth cup of the
Passover Supper. In Jewish homes it is filled with
wine but never drunk from.

Mother:

When Jesus took a cup after the supper, whether it
was the third, which was called the Eucharistic Cup,
or the fifth, which we call the Elijah Cup, and
announced to his disciples that it now contained "The
Blood of the Covenant" (Mk 14:24), the disciples
understood him.

Father:

The disciples were well versed in the fact that the children of Israel were sealed to the LORD God of Israel by "The Blood of the Covenant." When the covenant was to be ratified at Mount Sinai,

> Moses related to the people all the commanding words (commandments) of the LORD (YHWH) and all of the judgments. Then all of the people replied with one voice, saying "All of the commanding words that the LORD (YHWH) said, we will do!" (Ex 24:3).

Then Moses had twelve stone pillars set up to represent the twelve tribes and an altar built to represent God. Burnt offerings were made to God and bullocks were sacrificed as Peace offerings. Moses had the blood that was drained from the sacrifices placed in large basins. He took half of the blood and threw it upon the altar.

> He took the book of the covenant (commanding words) and read it to the listening people. And they said that "All that the LORD (YHWH) has said, we will hear and we will do." Then Moses took the remaining basins of blood and threw it onto all of the people, sealing them to God in the covenant. Moses announced, "Behold, the blood of the covenant which the LORD (YHWH) has cleaved Himself to you according to all of these commanding words" (Ex 24:8).

Mother:

Although the synoptic Gospels (Matthew, Mark and Luke) may seem to present a separate tradition from the fourth Gospel (John) concerning the origins of the Eucharist, the seemingly separate traditions are one. You cannot separate a covenant, whether it is the Sinai Covenant or the New Covenant (1 Cor 11:25) from its commandments. Moses had the Israelites vow obedience to the commandments before he sealed them to God with the blood covenant.

Consequently, the New Covenant proclaimed in the synoptics (Mt 26:28; Mk 14:24; Lk 22:20) and Paul (1 Cor 11:25) cannot be separated from the New Commandment found in the fourth Gospel (Jn 13:34,35):

I give to you a new commandment:
>   that you should love one another,
>   that you should love each other just as I have
>   loved you!
By this shall everyone know that you are my
>   disciples,
>   if you love one another.

Father:

Therefore, we cannot say that we are faithful to the New Covenant of Christ if we ignore his new commandment. We must "love one another" as our brothers and sisters in Christ. We are the children of the one God.

Mother and Father:

As our Afikoman, we will all now share this one "loaf" that was hidden from us and then found by us again. We will simply express in this sharing of bread the Agape-Love that we have for one another.

> Although we are many individuals, because of the one bread we are one body by sharing the one bread (1 Cor 10:17).

At this final breaking of bread, this simple and plain unleavened bread becomes a symbol of the life we all share intimately together in the love of Christ.

Father takes the two halves of the Afikoman. Taking a small piece for himself to eat, he passes the two halves to those seated on either side of the table.

As the Agape-Afikoman is shared, Father reads the following:

But be eager for the better gifts (charismata)
    and yet I will show you a more excellent way:

If I speak with the tongues of men and of the
        angels,
    but do not have love (Agape)
I have become as brass sounding or a cymbal
    clanging!

And if I prophesy,
and if I know all the mysteries and possess all
        knowledge,
and if I have all the faith necessary to remove
        mountains,
    but I do not have love (Agape)—
then I am nothing!

And if I give away all my goods to give food to the
        poor
and deliver up my body that I may be burned,
    but I do not have love (Agape),
I have gained nothing!

Love has patience,
    love is kind,
    it is not envious.
Love is not boastful nor puffed up,
    it is not indecent,
    nor seeks things for itself.
It is not easily provoked
    nor thinks evil of others.
It rejoices in truth,
    it covers all things,
    it believes in all things,
    places its hope in all things,
    and endures all things.

Love never fails:
    prophesying shall be done away with,
    speaking in tongues will cease,
    knowledge will fail us.

For now, we only know in part,
   and in part we prophesy.
But when the perfect state comes,
   then what we know only in part
   shall be done away with!

When I was a young child,
   I spoke as a young child,
   and thought as a young child.
But now that I am an adult
   I have put behind me those things of childhood.
Now we see things as a riddle in a darkened mirror,
   but then we shall see face to face!
I have only partial knowledge now,
   but then I shall know, just as I am known!

Of all the things that we have now,
   only these three will remain,
and they are faith, hope and love,
   but the greatest of all of these is agape-love!
   (1 Cor 13:1-13).

Mother:

Now we will all share the fifth cup of the seder, the
Elijah Cup. We will all share the Elijah Cup in our
simple Agape-Afikoman in respect for the new
covenant into which Christ sealed us to himself and
to each other with his own blood. For, just as Moses
sealed the children of Israel to God at Mount Sinai,
and to each other in a covenant relationship by
pouring the blood of the covenant upon the altar of
God and splashing the remaining onto the people (Ex
24:3-8), our Lord Jesus sealed us to himself and to
each other in the new covenant relationship of the
family of God by his own blood of the new covenant
(1 Cor 11:25).

Father sips from the Elijah Cup and passes it to those
around the table.

Father:

Beloved
    let us love each other,
    because love is of God
and everyone who loves
    has been born of God
    and knows God!

Anyone who is not a loving person
    has never known God
    because God is love.

The love of God was manifested to us in this way,
    God sent his only begotten son into the world
    that we might live through him!

In this love,
    it is not that we have loved God,
    but that he loves us so very much
and sent his son as the offering for our sins.

Beloved,
    if God has loved us so much
    we must also love each other.
For no one has ever seen God,
    yet, if we love each other
God resides within us
    and his love is perfected in us!

By this do we know that we reside in him
    and he in us,
    because of his spirit that he has given to us!

And we have seen and bear witness
    that the Father has sent the Son
    as the savior of the world.
Whoever confesses that Jesus is the Son of God
    God resides in that person and that person in
    God!

And we have known and have believed
    in this love which God has for us.

God is love
  and whoever remains in love
    dwells in God,
  and God dwells there within.

Love is perfected within us in this way,
  that we have confidence on the day of judgment,
for even as he was
  so we are also, in relation to this world.
There is no fear in love
  because perfect love casts out fear.
Fear has to do with punishment
  and love has not been made perfect in someone
    who fears!

We love him because he first loved us.
And if anyone should say that they love God
    and yet hates a brother or sister,
  that one is a liar!

For if someone does not love the brother or sister
    they see
  how can they love God whom they cannot see?

The commandment that we have from him is this:
  that by loving God, we also love our sisters and
    brothers! (1 Jn 4:7-21)

Peace and Blessing.

Pax et Bonum.

Paz y Bien.

Shalom u-Vrakhah.

Appendix

Pronouncing the Hebrew Prayers

The English transliteration of Hebrew—the writing of Hebrew using the English alphabet—is a common practice. It enable those who cannot read Hebrew to at least pronounce the Hebrew blessings.

Pronounce vowels as you might if your were speaking a Latin language (Spanish, Italian, etc.):

"a" is pronounced "ah" as in "father"

"e" (short) is pronounced "eh" as in "bell"
"e" (long) is pronounced "ay" as in "bay"

"i" is pronounced "ee" as in "machine"

"o" is pronounced "o" as in "go"

"u" is pronounced "oo" as in "blue"

Two vowel combinations must be carefully noted:

"ay" is pronounced like a long "i" as in "high"

"ey" is pronounced like a long "a" as in "bay"

In other vowel combinations, each vowel is pronounced separately. For example, "Israel" is pronounced "Yisra'el" (Yees-rah-ell).

All the consonants in Hebrew are pronounced like English consonants, including "y" as in "yellow." The "r" is properly pronounced as in Spanish or Italian, although in Israel one can hears it in conversation with a German, French, and Moroccan pronunciation.

The consonant combination "sh" is pronounced the same as in English. "Tz" is a little harder, pronounced "ts" as in "cats." Two others are usually quite difficult for Americans:

"kh" is pronounced "ch" as in the German "ach" or Scottish "loch"

"ch" is pronounced as the Spanish "j" as in "jota" or the Slavic "h."

In conversation, however, many Israelis pronounce "ch" the same as "kh" even though "ch" should be sounded in the throat and "kh" in the back of the mouth. If these two combinations are too difficult to master, pronounce both of them as the English "k."

After practicing these sounds for a while, try this sentence:

Barukh ata Adonay, Elohenu, melekh ha olam.

It should sound like:

Bah-rookh ahtah Ah-doe-Neigh, El-low-hay-noo, meh-lekh hah oh-lahm.

Now you are ready to try the seder blessings.

Lighting the Holy Day Lights (page 60):

Barukh ata Adonay, Elohenu, melekh ha olam,

(Blessed are you O LORD our God,
   the king of the universe,)

Asher kidshanu bemitzvotav

(that sanctified us by your commandments)

Vetzivanu lehadlik ner shel yom tov.

(and commanded us
to light the lights for the good day.)

Blessing the Fruit of the Vine (page 64):

Barukh ata Adonay, Elohenu, melekh ha olam,

(Blessed are you O LORD our God,
the king of the universe,)

Borey Pri ha Gafen.

(creator [of the] Fruit of the Vine.)

Blessing the Karpas (page 69):

Barukh ata Adonay, Elohenu, melekh ha olam,

(Blessed are you O LORD our God,
the king of the universe,)

Borey Pri ha Adamah.

(creator [of the] Fruit of the Earth.)

Invitation to Passover (page 70):

This invitation is actually spoken in Aramaic, the language Jesus spoke.

Ha lachma anya di akhalu avhatana

(Behold, the bread of poverty that was eaten by our
ancestors)

Be' arah de Mitzrayim.

(in the land of Egypt.)

Kol dikhfin yeytay veyekhol,

(All hungry come and eat,)

Kol ditzrik yaytay veyiFsach.

(All needy come and [join] our Passover.)

Hashatah hakhah, leshana haba'ah be arah
deYisra'el.

(Now we are here, in the year coming may we be in
the land of Israel.)

Hashatah avdey, leshana haba'ah, beney chorin!

(Now we are slaves, in the year coming may we be
free!)

Blessing the Bread, Ha-Motzi (pages 96, 97):

Barukh ata Adonay, Elohenu, melekh ha olam,

(Blessed are you O LORD our God,
the king of the universe,)

Ha motzi lechem min ha aretz.

(who brings forth bread from the earth.)

Blessing the Unleavened Bread (pages 97, 98):

Barukh ata Adonay, Elohenu, melekh ha olam,

(Blessed are you O LORD our God,
the king of the universe,)

Asher kidshanu bemitzvotav

(that sanctified us by your commandments)

Vetzivanu al akhilot Matzah.

(and commanded us concerning the eating of
unleavened bread.)

Blessing the Bitter Herb (page 99):

Barukh ata Adonay, Elohenu, melekh ha olam,

(Blessed are you O LORD our God,
the king of the universe,)

Asher kidshanu bemitzvotav

(that sanctified us by your commandments)

Vetzivanu al akhilot Maror.

(and commanded us concerning the eating of the
bitter herb.)

Give A Haggadah To Everyone Around Your Seder Table!

Everyone who participates in a Passover seder should have the opportunity to read the prayers and blessings along with the host.

Now you can provide your guests with individual Haggadahs, which they can use in the ritual and retain as a keepsake of their experience in your home or church.

This Haggadah is an exact reprinting of Part III of *Celebrating an Authentic Passover Seder*.

Save $15 by taking advantage of our "6-pack" discount:

$7.50 each
$30 for pack of six

**CELEBRATING
AN AUTHENTIC
PASSOVER SEDER:
A Participant's Haggadah
for Home and Church**

Joseph M. Stallings

Paper, 64 pages, 5½" x 8½"
ISBN 0-89390-297-7